ASSESSING STUDENT LEARNING IN THE COMMUNITY
AND TWO-YEAR COLLEGE

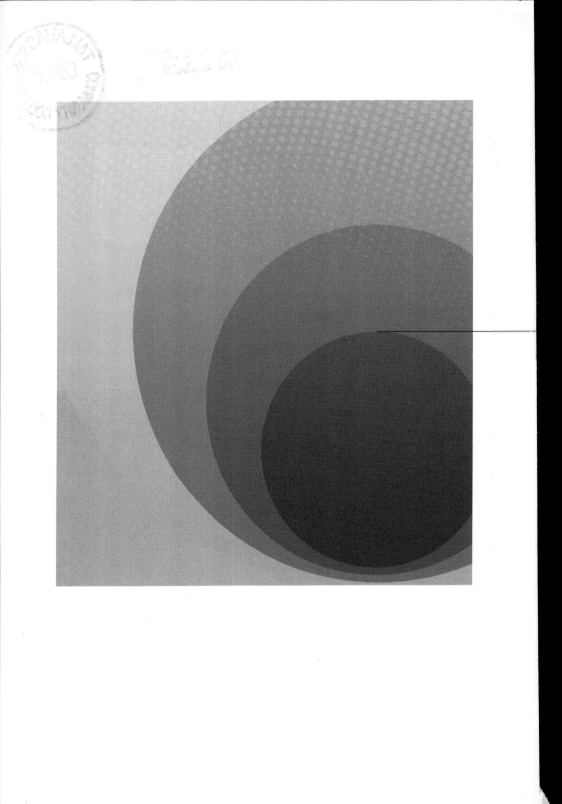

ASSESSING STUDENT LEARNING IN THE COMMUNITY AND TWO-YEAR COLLEGE

Successful Strategies and Tools Developed by
Practitioners in Student and Academic Affairs

EDITED BY

Megan Moore Gardner, Kimberly A. Kline,
and Marilee J. Bresciani

Foreword by William E. Piland

STERLING, VIRGINIA

COPYRIGHT © 2014 BY
STYLUS PUBLISHING, LLC.

Published by Stylus Publishing, LLC
22883 Quicksilver Drive
Sterling, Virginia 20166-2102

Library of Congress Cataloging-in-Publication Data
Assessing student learning in the community and two-
year college : successful strategies and tools developed
by practitioners in student and academic affairs / edited
by Megan Moore Gardner, Kimberly A. Kline, and
Marilee J. Bresciani.
    p.   cm. —
Includes bibliographical references and index.
ISBN 978-1-57922-911-5 (cloth : alk. paper)
ISBN 978-1-57922-912-2 (pbk. : alk. paper)
ISBN 978-1-57922-913-9 (library networkable e-edition)
ISBN 978-1-57922-914-6 (consumer e-edition)
1. Community colleges—United States—Evaluation.
I. Gardner, Megan Moore, 1976-
LB2331.63.A76 2013
378.1'543—dc23

                                        2013017341

13-digit ISBN: 978-1-57922-911-5 (cloth)
13-digit ISBN: 978-1-57922-912-2 (paperback)
13-digit ISBN: 978-1-57922-913-9 (library networkable e-edition)
13-digit ISBN: 978-1-57922-914-6 (consumer e-edition)

Printed in the United States of America

All first editions printed on acid-free paper
that meets the American National Standards Institute
Z39-48 Standard.

Bulk Purchases

Quantity discounts are available for use in workshops and for
staff development.
Call 1-800-232-0223

First Edition, 2014

10   9   8   7   6   5   4   3   2

This book is dedicated to the faculty, staff, and administrators at community and two-year colleges who strive to create centers of excellence for teaching and learning on their campuses. More specifically, we thank those who have contributed to the development of this book for sharing their wisdom and experiences. Their insights, ideas, and examples will greatly enhance the work of others engaged in assessing student learning and success at community and two-year institutions.

CONTENTS

Community colleges throughout the nation, for a number of years, have struggled mightily with the shift from an instructional to a learning paradigm. The development, implementation, and assessment of student learning outcomes (SLOs) have been problematic, particularly for faculty who do not teach in the career/technical areas of the curriculum. With much gnashing of teeth, community college faculty have focused on specifically what they want their students to learn and have developed the SLOs that drive learning. In many colleges, faculty have undergone professional development, held department and discipline discussions, and made the transformation from imparting knowledge through teacher-centric methods to focusing on student learning. Classroom implementation has been moving to more student-centered approaches to learning including cooperative learning, group projects, study groups, and cognitive-based approaches to constructing new knowledge.

Ah, but assessment of student learning remains the bugaboo. It has been difficult enough determining which SLOs have been obtained and to what degree in the classroom; moving to assessment of learning at the program, service, and institutional levels presents a whole new degree of difficulty. Some colleges assess learning through traditional measures such as end-of-unit teacher-made tests, pre- and posttests, department-wide tests, and the like. Other faculty members have used more authentic measures such as work sampling, online portfolios, presentations, and social media use to demonstrate learning. For student services providers, the assessment of these measures' impact on student learning is extremely challenging. The tried and not-so-true methods of counting the numbers of students who belong to clubs, visit the tutoring center, and meet with a counselor during the academic year will no longer suffice, nor will the "customer satisfaction" surveys of users of these services. These methods have nothing to do with an "assessment of learning."

Now, in one volume, comes a book with its sole emphasis on assessing student learning for community college practitioners. The timing for this book could not be better. With regional accrediting agencies across the country focusing on the assessment piece of the learning paradigm, with more and more states moving to a form of performance-based funding with specific milestones that equate to dollars for colleges, and with greater demands for meaningful accountability measures from state and federal sources, assessment has risen to the top of the priorities hierarchy for community colleges. The strategies and tools presented in this volume should be of assistance to community college instructional and student services professionals. CEOs, vice presidents, and deans are provided with ideas that can assist them as they view assessment from a global perch. Program and service directors, teaching faculty, counselors, and advisors who are on the front lines will learn assessment approaches that they can utilize from day one. This book also provides community college leaders with the tools to assess student learning for better-informed decision-making.

All colleges are moving toward a data-driven, decision-making culture. While colleges have always collected data about their students, such as demographics, progress through the institution, including retention, persistence and completion measures, now emphases are being placed on data concerning student learning. The completion agenda has forced community colleges to ascertain the amount of student success at the institution. For example, at one large California community college it was discovered that students who earned a grade of C, a passing grade, in the highest-level development math course had a 1-in-10 chance of earning a passing grade in college algebra. This information led to a total redesign of the math curriculum. Success rates for all students in college algebra, subsequently, increased. This change required an assessment of what students had learned and the degree to which they learned it.

A unique strength of this book is chapter 4, "Building a Professional Development Plan." College faculty and student support services personnel are not trained in assessment. Faculty members are steeped in the traditions and structures of their disciplines and student services professionals are taught the ins-and-outs of the nature and delivery of the services they provide. There is no intuitive schema professionals hold in their heads that leads them to sound assessment principles and practices. For working professionals, professional development, as explained in that chapter, is necessary to make the culture of evidence come alive in community colleges.

This compendium of work on assessing student learning will be especially valuable to all of those professionals who work in student support and service areas of community colleges. Often the connection between these vital support services and student learning is not recognized or valued within an academic institution. Assessing the impact of these support services on learning is vital, not only for improving these services, but for justifying their continued existence. Because these services often don't produce credits or directly lead to apportionment funding, they are the first ones cut during rough budgetary times. However, assessment of the impacts of these services on student learning is part of a comprehensive assessment strategy, as presented in this book.

William E. Piland
Professor Emeritus
San Diego State University

PREFACE

Megan Moore Gardner

T his book is designed to serve as a practical resource for community and two-year college professionals engaging in all levels of learning outcomes assessment in both academic and cocurricular environments. It is our intention that readers will garner insights that may be used to inform the creation of new assessment efforts or to enhance and strengthen those efforts already in motion on community and two-year college campuses. The book highlights significant components of the assessment experience beginning with the creation of a learning-centered culture and the effective development and articulation of the goals for assessment, followed by engagement in the "nuts and bolts" of various parts of the assessment process, and concludes with strategies for success and future considerations.

Woven into many of the chapters are examples from faculty and student affairs/services professionals at community and two-year colleges throughout the United States. A number of chapters also offer discussion points or questions that guide readers through a reflective and thoughtful process designed to inform their own work with assessment. Such activities and examples provide readers with concrete experiences that can or have actually occurred in a community or two-year college setting in an effort to demonstrate the opportunities and challenges posed at all parts of the assessment process and to assist them in the realization of their own assessment goals.

Outline of Chapters

This book consists of 11 chapters. The first chapter explores key questions to answer in order to engage in an effective assessment process and discusses how to establish a shared conceptual framework and common language that act as the foundation of the process. It also discusses what to document and how, as well as how the results will be used. Chapter 2 examines the need for and creation of a learning-centered institutional culture coupled with a commitment to evidence-based decision making. It discusses visioning, collaboration, communication, and garnering buy-in as tools for creating and sustaining such a culture. Chapter 3 describes how to establish shared learning outcomes and determine priorities for the assessment process and highlights strategies for engagement. Chapter 4 highlights the steps for establishing a professional development plan and situates those plans within the context of the community or two-year college setting.

Chapter 5 moves into the "nuts and bolts" section of the book, detailing how to develop and write assessment outcomes as well as how to utilize outcome mapping as a tool for effective assessment. Chapter 6 discusses data analysis and results interpretation, which is complemented by the discussion in chapter 7 about how to effectively use and communicate the results of an assessment process. Chapter 8 offers insight into using the results of assessment for decision making in both the curricular and cocurricular environments, and chapter 9 discusses how to use the results to inform program review and budgeting. Chapter 10 closes the loop with a discussion of ways to evaluate the assessment process and inform future practice. The book concludes with a discussion of future issues and considerations in chapter 11.

Selection of Chapter Authors

The editors insisted that each chapter be written with the input of at least one community or two-year college professional so that the information provided is both meaningful and applicable within the community and two-year college institutional culture. Institutional design, politics, resources, and stakeholders unique to these specific postsecondary institutions remained at the forefront of the emphasis of this book and were given voice through the eyes and experiences of each chapter's authors.

The authors hail from community, two-year, and four-year colleges throughout the United States and hold a variety of academic and administrative positions including senior-level leaders, academic and cocurricular administrators, assessment and institutional research directors, and faculty. The knowledge, experiences, thoughts, and ideas of these effective and recognized professionals have resulted in a comprehensive and informative resource that will be relevant both today and in the future.

ACKNOWLEDGMENTS

We wish to acknowledge the noteworthy efforts of the chapter authors and applaud them for their willingness to share their insights and experiences. We appreciate their honesty in sharing their assessment trials, tribulations, and tips for success in order to enhance and strengthen the work of others. Such insights will enable academic and student affairs/services professionals in community and two-year colleges to develop effective ways of demonstrating student growth and development in both the academic and cocurricular settings. We also wish to acknowledge the efforts of Julie Hykes from the University of Akron. Her attention to detail and commitment to this project resulted in an organized and efficient editing process.

I

DETERMINING WHAT YOU WANT TO GET OUT OF THE PROCESS

Megan Moore Gardner and Barbara Milliken

A key component of effective outcomes-based assessment for any institution of higher education is determining what you want to get out of the process. Such foresight will guide your assessment work and help you establish organizational priorities. Before establishing the desired outcomes, however, it is first necessary to determine why you are engaged in the assessment process and how outcomes-based assessment can contribute to the realization of your overall institutional goals and success. Once you have determined the reasons underlying your engagement in the assessment process, you must work to decrease barriers to establishing a shared conceptual framework and common language that permeate the organization and contribute to organizational learning and growth.

We begin this chapter by defining *outcomes-based assessment*, differentiating it from both research and evaluation, and discuss why such assessment is necessary and important to higher education. We then discuss the push for accountability in community and two-year colleges as well as how assessment may be used to inform organizational improvement and accountability efforts. Next, we argue for the need to establish a shared conceptual framework and highlight ways to enhance trust and increase collaboration. In addition, we discuss the importance of making assessment a top-down priority; incorporating it into testing, advising, and remediation efforts; using it in response to employer demands; and incentivizing student success. Additionally, we look at student success through career pathways and outline how and why to involve stakeholders. Finally, we share key issues to consider when determining how assessment results will be used; discuss navigating institutional and community politics; highlight the importance of transparency; and argue for linking assessment to strategic planning, budgeting, and resource allocation in an effort to improve overall student learning and development.

What Is Outcomes-Based Assessment?

A number of definitions for *outcomes-based assessment* exist. Regardless of differences in the scope or the foundation, outcomes-based assessment is always about improving student success in both the academic and cocurricular settings (Bresciani, Moore Gardner, & Hickmott, 2009; Palomba & Banta, 1999; Schuh, Upcraft, & Associates, 2001). This book utilizes the definition presented by Bresciani (2006). She defines *outcomes-based assessment* as a systematic and intentional process during which higher education professionals

> articulate what the program intends to accomplish in regard to its services, research, student learning, and faculty/staff development programs. The faculty and/or professionals then purposefully plan the program so that the intended results (e.g., outcomes) can be achieved; implement methods to systematically—over time—identify whether end results *have* been achieved; and, finally, use the results to plan improvements or make recommendations for policy consideration, recruitment, retention, resource reallocation, or new resource requests. This systematic process of evaluation is then repeated at a later date to determine whether the program improvements contribute to intended outcomes. (p. 14)

The outcomes of such assessment are used to enhance and improve student learning at the program, department, divisional, and/or institutional level.

When outcomes-based assessment is utilized effectively, the results may inform strategic planning, budgeting, and overall student learning and development efforts at community and two-year colleges. To truly understand outcomes-based assessment, however, it is necessary to differentiate assessment from evaluation and research. Schuh, Upcraft, and Associates (2001) suggest that evaluation involves efforts on the part of higher education professionals to utilize assessment evidence to improve organizational effectiveness. Palomba and Banta (1999) concur and argue that assessment results should be intentionally communicated if they are to be of use in institutions of higher education. In accordance with the insights of these authors, evaluation serves as a means to use assessment results in meaningful and significant ways.

Research and assessment, on the other hand, differ in both focus and scope. Research informs the development of theories and tests ideas, whereas assessment informs practice (Schuh et al., 2001). The results of assessment, then, are typically institution or practice specific whereas research is broader in scope and may be applied to the field in general. Research is often utilized when developing learning outcomes and developing educational experiences designed to yield specific outcomes. According to Bresciani et al. (2009), "Research may also be used to help interpret the application of the findings. However, programmatic outcomes-based assessment may rarely follow strict research methodology. While institutional outcomes-based assessment may follow strict research methodology, the findings may still not be generalizable" (p. 19).

Why Is Outcomes-Based Assessment Important?

Community and two-year colleges are currently faced with many challenges including erosion of public confidence resulting in increased demands for accountability by internal and external stakeholders, shrinking capital and human resources, and larger and more diverse numbers of students choosing postsecondary education. Exacerbating these challenges are the unique, and sometimes mutually exclusive, needs of the collegiate, vocational, and continuing education programs offered under the umbrella of the community or two-year college; increased numbers of remedial course offerings; administration and faculty who are stretched too thin; and an overall disdain for external accountability demands at not only state and federal levels, but also at the local community level (Cohen & Brawer, 2008). Additionally, faculty at all institutional types were historically looked to as primarily responsible for demonstrating student learning. Today, however, both academic and student affairs/services professionals are expected not only to articulate but also to demonstrate the value and impact of academic and cocurricular experiences on overall student learning and development.

Kuh, Kinzie, Schuh, Whitt, and Associates (2005) argued that background characteristics and specific institutional type have less of an impact on students' learning and development than do the activities in which students are engaged during their postsecondary experiences. Further, the amount of time spent engaged in an activity, coupled with the level of effort applied by students in both academic and cocurricular settings, significantly impacts the growth and development of those students. Moreover, the manner in which a college or university utilizes resources and develops learning experiences that are of interest and of benefit to students significantly impacts overall growth and development (Kuh et al., 2005). Outcomes-based assessment may be used to inform resource allocations and highlight those services and experiences not only in which students are interested but also in which students actively engage and learn.

Accountability for Student Learning and Development

A review of higher education assessment literature demonstrates an increased emphasis on accountability with each passing year (Bresciani, 2006; Bresciani et al., 2009; Palomba & Banta, 1999; Schuh et al., 2001; Upcraft & Schuh, 1996). Increases in tuition and fees not matched by financial aid offerings, complex articulation agreements, and growing dissatisfaction with the quality and level of classroom instruction are just a few of the factors contributing to the public's disenchantment with the postsecondary educational enterprise (Bresciani et al., 2009; Cohen & Brawer, 2008; Palomba & Banta, 1999; Upcraft & Schuh, 1996). Outcomes-based assessment provides "quality assurance" and informs external accountability (Bresciani, 2006, p. 13). It yields information about where and how learning is fostered in both academic and cocurricular postsecondary environments.

A major reason for engaging in outcomes-based assessment in community and two-year colleges is to demonstrate the relevance and worth of programs and services in a time of shrinking resources (Palomba & Banta, 1999; Upcraft & Schuh, 1996). Schuh (2009) posits, "Colleges and universities increasingly are being asked to demonstrate how they make a difference in the lives of students, how they contribute to the economic development of their communities and states, and how they contribute to the national welfare" (p. 2). Outcomes-based assessment serves as a means to demonstrate how all facets of the postsecondary learning enterprise contribute to overall student learning and development and benefit the greater good. Bresciani et al. (2009) noted that the results of outcomes-based assessment may be used to inform the rationale for programs and services as well as to validate financial and human capital expenditures.

Astin (1991) suggested that "an institution's assessment practices are a reflection of its values" (p. 3). Student learning and development are at the center of any college or university mission and, therefore, serve as the guiding principles of the majority of academic and student affairs work. The results of outcomes-based assessment help with the communication of those values and demonstrate how the mission and values of an institution are or are not integrated into the fabric of its programs and services. Such assessment contributes to a culture of continuous improvement and the creation of *learning organizations* (Senge, 1990), or organizations in which the members are committed to public learning and continuous discourse about ways of knowing and doing within the organization.

Establishing a Shared Conceptual Framework

Banta, Jones, and Black (2009) note, "Effective assessment doesn't just happen. It emerges over time as an outcome of thoughtful planning, and in the spirit of continuous improvement, it evolves as reflection on the processes of implementing and sustaining assessment suggests modifications" (p. 3). To ensure the assessment process is one that is designed to be sustained over time and yield relevant and useful results, it is first necessary to create a shared conceptual framework and common language within and among those stake-holders who will be involved. A shared conceptual framework provides direction for the assessment process; is mission-driven and informed by research; and, like the assessment process itself, should be continually evaluated and modified when necessary. When fostered thoughtfully, a shared conceptual framework provides a sense of commonality and coherence with an institution, a department, or a program (Senge, 1990).

Key to the development of a strong conceptual framework for the assessment process is the removal of common barriers to collaboration and coherence within an organization. There are three commonly cited obstacles that higher education professionals attempting to engage in effective outcomes-based assessment may face: (a) a lack of time, (b) inadequate resources, and (c) limited understanding of assessment (Banta & Associates, 2002; Banta et al., 2009; Bresciani, 2006; Bresciani, Zelna, & Anderson, 2004; Palomba & Banta, 1999; Suskie, 2004; Upcraft & Schuh, 1996). Each can contribute to dissonance among members of an organization and serve to sabotage the process of creating a shared conceptual framework. Additionally, Bresciani et al. (2009) identified two barriers, trust and management of expectations, that stood out in the cocurricular setting that must also be considered when building cohesion among all members of a community or two-year college.

Trust and Collaboration

According to Bresciani et al. (2009), the issue of trust includes an inability of faculty to trust professionals outside of traditional academic roles to be valid contributors to the assessment of student learning and development, as well as concerns by faculty about how results are derived and used. Cohen and Brawer (2008) suggest, "The way colleges are organized leads most staff members to resist measurement of learning outcomes" (p. 214). Such resistance is due to the fact that a significant portion of community and two-year colleges that rely on course-specific, criterion-referenced measurement that examines learning against a particular predetermined standard would then be forced to shift gears and move to a more normative model that would be non-course-specific and require more patience and skill to construct a holistic and collaborative assessment process. Bresciani et al. (2009) advise,

> It is important to remember to make the process of how data will be used to inform decisions and who will use that data for decisions as public as possible. Doing so will begin to reduce anxiety and demonstrate evidence of consistent behavior. Only over time, through consistent behavior, will trust be established. (pp. 141–142)

When considering the role of student assessment within any institution, it is imperative to view the entire campus as a single evolving learning community (Darby, 2009). Although student assessment in its broadest sense has traditionally been seen as the responsibility of faculty within the context of the classroom, that narrow perspective is wholly insufficient for today's community and two-year college student. The complexity of offerings, coupled with the growing diversity of the student base, dictates a more holistic perspective of student assessment of learning. Nonacademic tasks traditionally deemed the responsibility of student services departments are being introduced and reinforced in the classroom, while professional and academic supports are layered among collaborative units consisting of curricular and cocurricular entities. Darby (2009) stresses the need for academics to expand their perspective of student assessment. She states that responsibility for learning exists outside of the classroom, and, therefore, responsibility for assessing learning also exists outside of the classroom.

If an organization is not careful, assessment can easily become the sole responsibility of the Institutional Research area, with "applicable" segments parceled out to identified entities. This chunked approach to communication might at first be appreciated by those individuals who are already feeling overwhelmed or stressed by the current student load, and for whom "tell me what I need to know" seems to be a more efficient method. However, this fractionalizing feeds into the silo effect that is so often apparent in higher education. Manning, Kinzie, and Schuh (2006) speak to this disconnected approach to assessment when describing the bureaucratic nature of educational organizations. This bureaucracy consists of highly specialized departments, at times a department of one or two people, with specifically outlined job descriptions. Such narrowing of responsibilities, in turn, leads to a scenario in which "services offered through various offices do not overlap and communication is limited or nonexistent" (p. 60). Faculty and staff who are attempting to navigate this type of system can find themselves on a convoluted fact-finding mission, which can easily undermine student success.

However, if an institution operates from the assumption that all administrators, faculty, and staff are invested in student success, it then becomes important for all entities to see the significance of their individual roles. An old parable about blind men and an elephant is applicable to this situation. Six blind men are all touching various parts of an elephant, and each one describes the elephant based on what he knows in that moment. For instance, one compares it to a wall (the side), a snake (the trunk), a rope (the tail), a tree (the knee), a spear (a tusk), and a fan (an ear). The moral of this story is that unless you are able to view something in its entirety, your perspective can be profoundly skewed.

To avoid perpetuating a segmented perspective that can lead to inconsistent priorities, ineffective initiatives, or even turf wars, it is important that there be a commonly shared strategic plan that ensures broad-based and well-defined responsibilities for conducting and/or responding to student assessment. Timely assessment can be a powerful motivator for buy-in and change. When performance is assessed on an ongoing basis and individuals are empowered to institute change based on feedback, the cycle of continuous improvement is put into motion. For example, Stark State College has a very thoughtfully designed strategic plan that clearly aligns the institution's stated values with goals, strategic objectives, and measures that encompass all facets of the organization (Addison et al., 2012). All faculty, staff, and administrators are asked to clearly identify how they personally contribute to supporting the strategic plan. A plan has been suggested to assign accountability for follow-through during individuals' annual performance evaluation. This strategic plan mirrors what the institution has declared as priorities for quality improvement as identified through the Academic Quality Improvement Program process, thus inviting investment and input from all areas of the institution.

Making Assessment a Top-Down Priority

Today's community or two-year college is a complex organization whose core mission encompasses terminal as well as transferable degrees, vocational education, community initiatives, lifelong learning, industry-specific job training, and more. The student assessment process is complex and has evolved in kind, resulting in curricular and cocurricular collaborations. In fact, inclusion of cocurricular components ensures that students' learning is enhanced through contextual experiences, contemplation, reflection, emotional engagement, and information acquisition (Keeling, 2004). If we can agree that learning takes place both within and outside of the classroom, then it follows that assessment of that learning should be derived from multiple sources. Examples might include clinical supervisors, internship coordinators, and professional mentors.

Darby (2009) describes two basic methods of cocurricular assessment. Simply stated, new programs can be developed in response to an identified need for skill development, or existing programs can be altered to allow for expanded opportunities for experiential learning. Beyond the classroom, service-learning, student government, community service and engagement, co-ops and internships, peer tutoring, and mentoring programs offer rich opportunities for meaningful, skill-specific assessment.

Although the assessment process is transferred to individuals other than faculty, the responsibility for establishing the metrics for assessment as well as the assessment methods may still lie with the individual faculty member or program director. Moreover, involving key institutional leaders from both academic and cocurricular realms in the assessment process will contribute to the creation of a shared language, increase transparency, and assist in the demolition of commonly constructed silos of communication that may exist within an organization. Providing a unified front regarding the extent to which engagement in assessment is expected, how results will be used, and how resources will be prioritized and allocated before, during, and after the assessment process will contribute to an overall sense of shared responsibility and a community-focused assessment process. According to Bresciani et al. (2009),

> The ability to focus on your locus of control can help clarify issues of trust and empower practitioners to see where they have the ability to influence interpretation of data, process, and policy and where they do not. The act of simply acknowledging that fact can demystify the process for many and encourage others to engage in the process with clarity of expectations. (pp. 142–143)

Assessment informs accountability efforts and provides institutional leaders with data to create reasonable expectations about what can or cannot be accomplished with available resources (Bresciani, 2006; Bresciani et al., 2009; Palomba & Banta, 1999). In turn, management of expectations is important when planning to engage in assessment and, more specifically, when working to develop a shared conceptual framework. Therefore, it is necessary for organizational leaders to work to create a conceptual framework that is based on trust and available human and capital resources, and that seeks results that can be systematically identified and measured.

Testing, Advising, and Remediation

In the typical community or two-year college environment, one may observe multiple groups charged with segmented responsibilities, but operating with inconsistent communication processes. The average student walks through the door and is very soon scheduled to sit for an entrance examination. Those results follow the student to an academic adviser who assists with scheduling classes based on those scores as they relate to an identified major. That choice of major may or may not be based on a career assessment, knowledge of the industry, or realistic employment prospects. Decisions related to credit hours may be made with little or no consideration of work or family expectations. The need to access support measures is often not anticipated and is considered only as a reaction to a critical academic situation. If the student is not successful, what career options are available to the student? Might attempts at remediation or changes in major negatively impact the student's standards of academic progress? How is a student to know? The questions continue with growing uncertainty at each juncture. But, underscoring all of them is the question, who is responsible for supporting student success? These diverse assessments congeal and may lead to frustration and unfulfilled goals (Cohen & Brawer, 2008).

One example of the collaborative paradigm is the initial assessment of students through entrance examinations. These can be impacted by the following:

- Institutional research, which identifies standard cutoff scores for course entry
- Registration, which determines the testing environment, time, and availability
- Admissions, which helps to interpret the scoring and remediation needs
- The career center, which supports career path decisions, based, in part, on entrance test scores and career assessments
- Financial aid, which not only determines funding eligibility, but also counsels students in the prudent management of resources

It is important to note that these determinations, based on assessment, generally occur prior to entering the classroom and continue to influence a student's progression throughout his or her tenure at the institution. In response, the National Academic Advising Association has come out in strong support of *intrusive advising*. This involves faculty and staff establishing relationships with students as early as possible, making referrals prior to the point where students are at risk of failure, and generally being a consistent resource and positive presence in students' lives (Cannon, 2013). In the end, it is the curricular assessment, in collaboration with a comprehensive cocurricular infrastructure, that will provide the foundational framework for success.

Community College Response to Employer Demands

The need for multiple sources of assessment and accountability may stem from the increased focus on core professional competencies. For example, advisory boards and employers across all industries resolutely demand enhanced soft skills for new hires. There is escalating intolerance for issues related to time management, dress, phone skills, ineffective communication across generations, accountability, and critical thinking. These soft skills are often highlighted in student codes of conduct or addressed in career development initiatives sponsored on campus.

In an effort to more fully enhance the generalization of these skills, some institutions, such as Stark State College, are choosing to include them as general learning outcomes noted on each and every syllabus. The classroom milieu can support professional expectations in regard to written and verbal speech, eye contact and nonverbal communication, accountability for absences, and critical thinking, among others. While consistency and continuity are easier to achieve in professional-track programs, especially among cohort groups, this growing outcry for enhanced soft skills by employers demands institutional investment. The community and two-year college must provide consistent reinforcement of standards of behavior with multiple opportunities for feedback. Well-designed program learning outcomes that are sensitive to professional behaviors become necessary to mold the next generation of employed professionals.

Incentivizing Student Success

Completion rates for students at public two- and four-year institutions are low, hovering around 20% and 57%, respectively (National Center for Education Statistics, 2013). While most states continue to fund their colleges and universities based on enrollment numbers, three states, Ohio, Indiana, and Tennessee, are stepping forward to incentivize schools for persistence and completion. As more states explore alternate funding models, it is expected that a resulting outcome will be the development of broad student support, sensitive and meaningful career assessment and advising, and a connected flow of information both within and among institutions. The Institute for a Competitive Workforce, in conjunction with the U.S. Chamber of Commerce (2012), addresses this issue and provides a performance overview in *Leaders & Laggards: A State-by-State Report Card on Public Postsecondary Education*.

Student Success Through Career Pathways

The concept of career pathways is a dominant theme in today's community and two-year college environment. Greater collaborations are noted between high schools and community or two-year colleges, as well as between those institutions and universities, with the goal of providing a seamless transition for students pursuing a career path that can begin with some college credit and progress to an industry-recognized certification, one-year credit certificate, associate's degree, bachelor's degree, and beyond. The basic role of the community or two-year college system has developed so as to provide not only career-specific associate degrees, but also a cost-effective option for transferable associate of science and associate of arts degrees. Furthermore, community and two-year colleges are currently working with universities to develop 3+1 programs. In these instances, partnering universities provide 300-level courses on the college campus, and at times at an adjusted tuition rate. Not only do students have an opportunity to save money, but they may not need to leave the comfort of the community or two-year college environment until they transfer to the university for the senior year. These innovative scheduling and collaboration practices aim to increase the number of students who continue along a career path and advance their academic goals.

High school students who participate in dual credit and early college programs are exiting high school with as few as 3–6 college credits or may even have a completed associate's degree at the time of graduation. One example of the impact of these programs is from Stark County, Ohio, where in 2010, 92% of the high school–based dual credit students earned 6,366 hours of college credit with a grade of C or better, with a financial benefit of $860,000 to $5,000,000, depending on the transfer of this credit (Rochford, O'Neill, Gelb, & Ross, 2010). The success of this program invites a top-down investment, which includes the board of regents, the Department of Education, boards of trustees, among others. The proven academic achievement of these students makes them attractive candidates to move into the university system, potentially maximizing the success rates of postsecondary institutions.

Involving Stakeholders

The previous examples of successful collaborations highlight the need to establish collective goals with engaged stakeholders. Bresciani et al. (2009) outline the significance of effectively communicating to those individuals who are affected by any assessment initiative. It is important to be sensitive to the sheer volume of student engagements that are occurring daily in the student services areas. Additionally, when setting expectations for faculty, remember that, particularly for full-time faculty, their responsibilities are extended far outside of the classroom. Their duties can include acting as student advisers; developing the curriculum; serving on standing committees, ad hoc committees, and advisory boards; engaging in club advising; and more. Of note is the fact that there are few opportunities for the typical faculty or staff member to participate in skill building as it relates specifically to student assessment and engagement.

Throughout the community and two-year college environment, the functions of academic programs are dictated by accrediting bodies, at both the program and institutional level. These entities mandate the institutionalization and utilization of continuous feedback systems. Although a typical exercise in generating a SWOT (strengths, weaknesses, opportunities, and threats) analysis might highlight timely key issues, it does not provide pointed feedback to targeted audiences and hold those entities accountable for positive gains. To capture more timely and pertinent information, a range of internal and external stakeholders are sought out for their feedback, utilizing a mix of institution-specific and nationally normed instruments. Examples of how institutions might enhance engagement are as follows:

- Link engagement to annual reviews.
- Include engagement as an element in the application for advancement in rank.
- Allow for leadership opportunities when moving initiatives forward.
- Support professional development related to student assessment through the teaching and learning department.

An example of focused skill enhancement takes place at Stark State College through a cross-divisional faculty and staff professional development team named BRIDGE (Building Relationships, Integrating Divisions, Generating Excellence). This team begins each year by reviewing significant institutional cocurricular assessment results and looks for opportunities to enhance outcomes through carefully crafted professional development activities scheduled throughout the academic year. Stakeholders from across the college, particularly those who undertake unique initiatives, are afforded opportunities to lead breakout sessions at retreats, conduct brown-bag sessions, or lead group discussion activities. A theme for the year is determined and then researched to identify best practices, which are then adapted to the needs of the institution and incorporated into progressive interactive teaching and learning events. This example highlights one of many mechanisms for engaging stakeholders and empowering them to have institutional impact.

Determining How the Results Will Be Used

The list of stakeholders for the community and two-year college varies little from that of the typical university. Internally, they remain the same: executive staff, deans, department chairs and coordinators, faculty, student services staff, building and grounds staff, and all support staff. Recently, a survey was conducted in preparation for a student persistence initiative that asked students to identify their academic supports. One student responded that each day when he entered the cafeteria, an employee there asked him about his day and gave gentle encouragement. He credited this woman with his determination to persist when he was otherwise tempted to withdraw. This story underscores the need to step back and reconsider perceptions of institutional resources.

External stakeholders of colleges and universities remain very similar as well: boards of regents, boards of trustees, regional accrediting bodies, program accrediting bodies, professional organizations, advisory boards, chambers of commerce, workforce investment boards, local career and technical centers, high schools, regional consortiums, and students' family members. While the community or two-year college may spend more time focusing on supporting the workforce needs of the state and local regions, universities tend to assume a broader reach, with greater emphasis on the national and global trends.

Key Questions to Consider

Each stakeholder group has its own unique perspective and skill sets. Stakeholders have the potential to contribute to, or thwart, the strategic design of an assessment project. When engaging stakeholders, The Pell Institute for the Study of Opportunity in Higher Education (2013) recommends engaging those who can do the following:

- Enhance the credibility of your assessment.
- Provide technical guidance.
- Guide daily operations.
- Either have, or be empowered with, some degree of influence related to execution.
- Have the ability to access funding.

Bresciani et al. (2009) suggest the following questions for selecting the most impactful stakeholders for each step of the process:

1. What individuals, groups, offices, or departments might be affected by the outcomes-based assessment process?
2. How might the representatives from such groups contribute to the outcomes-based assessment process?
3. What other stakeholders can be partnered with to develop and implement an effective outcomes-based assessment process?
4. What resources are available to promote and secure acceptance and involvement by stakeholders?

5. What resources and insights might our stakeholders provide for the outcomes-based assessment process?
6. What is the best use of stakeholder time and talent during the outcomes-based assessment process, and how can we maximize the use of each? (pp. 72–73)

Considering Organizational Politics/Culture

Community college leaders are tasked with interpreting assessment data, and then making strategic decisions to enhance the teaching and learning experience. This generally involves the board of trustees, which may consist of business professionals, as opposed to educators. It follows that there can be some inherent challenges to developing shared perspectives of timelines, decision making, and accountability as the board members are tasked with operational and fiduciary decision making.

The adage that change occurs at the "speed of business" simply cannot be applied to the traditional institution of higher education. For example, in business, decision-making capability can lie with a single individual. Managers are leaders who are solely held accountable for productivity, often assessed by the financial bottom line. By contrast, higher education tends to have layers of stakeholders who are given a voice in the nature and direction of chosen initiatives. Additionally, the assessment of projects, and labeling them as either successful or unsuccessful, may have limited or indirect impact on budgets, making them difficult to quantify.

A community or two-year college's reliance on shared governance, which moves new policies and procedures through a series of committees, can frustrate those who are accustomed to operating within a much more condensed decision-making structure. In spite of the slowed response time, shared governance, if practiced in good faith, invites investment and adherence and can generate a quality product that more sensitively considers the nuances of a particular institution. Analysis of assessment data flows from the governance committees to the college leadership for final review. Although the efficiency and efficacy of any institution's shared governance process might be a source of debate, this pathway to policy-making ensures that the collective voice of the faculty and staff has been heard.

Transparency

To ensure that the aforementioned collective voice of faculty and staff is heard, as well as to minimize common concerns about how assessment results will be used, it is important that community and two-year college assessment leaders maintain transparency as a top priority in the assessment process. Transparency within an organization invites a top-down investment in quality improvement. The analysis of assessment data through the lens of continuous improvement leads to the development of initiatives that support both institutional and program accreditations. There is obvious account-ability for outcomes by individuals assuming leadership roles throughout the institution. Operating within this transparent model of data sharing allows for enhanced feelings of empowerment, which can help front-line faculty and staff to manage any anxiety they may experience as a result of concern that data could be used punitively.

Despite obvious concerns, dissection of negative data remains a call to action. Use of the shared governance model is an accepted vehicle for reporting on the status of initiatives, gaining support for new strategies, and enhancing accountability. One key to the successful management of assess-ment data is communication of information related to outcomes and result-ing plans of action. This minimizes the mistrust that may arise when faculty and staff fear the management of negative data and further supports the organizational goal for transparency. The methods of communication (i.e., e-mail, newsletters, department meetings, or public forums) are less signifi-cant than the honest act of communication itself.

What might the ramifications be of negative data? Beware of turning people away from becoming more involved in the larger institution. Sensitive data management and communication means avoiding pointing to a single identifiable person or subset of individuals when noting failings. Instead, this can be an opportunity to support cross training and professional development, or to access external resources that might not have otherwise been available.

Link to Strategic Planning, Budgeting, and Resource Allocation

Linking assessment to resource allocation, budgeting, and strategic planning is discussed in depth in other chapters within this book. However, it is impor-tant to note here that community and two-year college professionals must stress the need to link the gathering and dissemination of assessment results to an outcomes-based assessment cycle as part of the strategic planning, budget-ing, and resource allocation processes. This requires careful review of what assessments are already in place and a commitment to embracing continuous measures to inform decision making, as opposed to status snapshots.

Prioritizing, establishing timelines, determining measurable objectives, and tracking progress all invite data-driven resource allocation. Although it is not necessary to address each and every area of need immediately, the creation of a data-based strategic plan, budgeting, and resource allocation system does result in well-reasoned strategies with continuous measurement of success.

Conclusion

As noted in the opening paragraph of this chapter, determining what you want out of the assessment process is important for creating and sustaining effective outcomes-based assessment. Consideration of such factors as organizational culture, resources, stakeholder expectations, and leadership structure will inform the assessment process and assist in the establishment of institutional priorities. By developing a shared commitment to and understanding of both assessment and organizational priorities for assessment among members of your organization, you will contribute to the creation of a shared conceptual framework and common language that will result in organizational learning and growth. More significantly, a strong foundation of transparency, commitment, and shared knowledge will enhance the student experience and augment holistic student learning and development on your campus.

References

Addison, M., David, J., Gibson-Shreve, L., Janson, P., Komer, G., Messner, M. B., . . . Zerbe, M. (2012). *Stark State College strategic plan 2011–2013: Optimizing opportunities. 2012–2013 update*. North Canton, OH: Stark State College.

Astin, A. (1991). *Assessment for excellence: The philosophy and practice of assessment and evaluation in higher education*. New York, NY: Macmillan.

Banta, T., & Associates. (2002). *Building a scholarship of assessment*. San Francisco, CA: Jossey-Bass.

Banta, T., Jones, E., & Black, K. (2009). *Designing effective assessment: Principles and profiles of good practice*. San Francisco, CA: Jossey-Bass.

Bresciani, M. J. (2006). *Outcomes-based academic and co-curricular program review: A compilation of institutional review practices*. Sterling, VA: Stylus.

Bresciani, M. J., Moore Gardner, M., & Hickmott, J. (2009). *Demonstrating student success: A practical guide to outcomes-based assessment of learning and development in student affairs*. Sterling, VA: Stylus.

Bresciani, M., Zelna, C., & Anderson, J. (2004). *Assessing student learning and development: A handbook for practitioners*. Washington, DC: National Association of Student Personnel Administrators.

Cannon, J. (2013). Intrusive advising 101: How to be intrusive without intruding. *Academic Advising Today, 36*(1). Retrieved from http://www.nacada.ksu .edu/Resources/Academic-Advising-Today/View-Articles/Intrusive-Advising -101-How-to-be-Intrusive-Without-Intruding.aspx

Cohen, A., & Brawer, F. (2008). *The American community college.* San Francisco, CA: Jossey-Bass.

Darby, S. (2009). *Assessment: Shared responsibility at Stark State College* [PowerPoint slides]. Presentation to Stark State College on May 12, 2009. Retrieved from https://www.starkstate.edu/luminis/files/facadvise/assessment/

Keeling, R. P. (Ed.). (2004). *Learning reconsidered: A campus-wide focus on the student experience.* Washington, DC: National Association of Student Personnel Administrators and American College Personnel Association.

Kuh, G., Kinzie, J., Schuh, J., Whitt, E., & Associates. (2005). *Student success in college: Creating conditions that matter.* San Francisco, CA: Jossey-Bass.

Manning, K., Kinzie, J., & Schuh, J. (2006). *One size does not fit all: Traditional and innovative models of student affairs practice.* New York, NY: Routledge.

National Center for Education Statistics. (2013). *The condition of education.* Retrieved from http://nces.ed.gov/programs/coe/indicator_cva.asp

Palomba, C., & Banta T. (1999). *Assessment essentials: Planning, implementing, and improving assessment in higher education.* San Francisco, CA: Jossey-Bass.

The Pell Institute for the Study of Opportunity in Higher Education, the Institute for Higher Education Policy, and Pathways to College Network. (2013). *Engage stakeholders & select a team.* Retrieved from http://toolkit.pellinstitute.org/evaluation-guide/plan-budget/engage-stakeholders/

Rochford, J. A., O'Neill, A., Gelb, A., & Ross, K. J. (2010). *Growth & impact: The expansion of high school based dual credit in Stark County, Ohio.* Retrieved from http://www.edpartner.org/pdfs/Growth_&_Impact.pdf

Schuh, J. (2009). *Assessment methods for student affairs.* San Francisco, CA: Jossey-Bass.

Schuh, J., Upcraft, M., & Associates. (2001). *Assessment practice in student affairs: An applications manual.* San Francisco, CA: Jossey-Bass.

Senge, P. (1990). *The fifth discipline. The art and practice of the learning organization.* New York, NY: Doubleday.

Suskie, L. (2004). *Assessing student learning: A common sense guide.* Bolton, MA: Anker.

Upcraft, M., & Schuh, J. (1996). *Assessment in student affairs: A guide for practitioners.* San Francisco: Jossey-Bass.

U.S. Chamber of Commerce. (2012). *Leaders & laggards: A state-by-state report card on public postsecondary education.* Retrieved from http://icw.uschamber.com/reportcard/

2

ESTABLISHING A LEARNING-CENTERED CULTURE

Commitment to Evidence-Based Decision Making

Paul A. Dale

The path of least resistance and least trouble is a mental rut already made. It requires troublesome work to undertake the alternation of old beliefs. —John Dewey

Before one can ponder, describe, or even prescribe how to implement and operationalize a learning-centered culture—often a presumed state in community colleges—it is critically important to look at the core values that provide a launching point for long-term cultural commitment. These values serve as enablers of organizational change in order to fully realize evidence-based decision making and learning-centered leadership. More important, these core organizational values increase the probability of a culture consistently yielding high levels of student learning and success. Dewey (1927) drives at the crux of instilling organizational culture when he suggests the laborious and challenging nature of altering beliefs, in this case, a commitment to learning-centered practices. This deep commitment to the relentless pursuit of improving student learning, while paramount and expected, is just plain hard work.

The purpose of this chapter is to provide advice on and experiential examples of how to implement; maintain; and, most important, sustain a learning-centered culture. To fully understand a learning-centered culture in a community college, focus must be placed on the elements and practice of visioning, collaboration, communication, and building long-term support and buy-in.

Discussion about creating a learning-centered culture must first begin with a look, albeit brief, at three core cultural values that are essential for a learning-centered college to flourish: efficacy of multiple webs of interdependence, appreciation of organizational hard work, and optimization of functional performance. The origin of these cultural values lies in systems thinking and systems theory. Without this working cultural foundation, the elements of a learning-centered college will not take root, germinate, or produce the levels of commitment that will yield significant learning year after year.

First, a structural cultural core marker that enables a community college to be truly learning centered is the valuing of multiple webs of interdependence, collaboration, and the desire to mobilize and engage a broad range of faculty and staff from across the college. The diversity of perspectives found in all community college organizational divisions and units allows leadership to triangulate points of view and engage multiple elements of the organization. Organizations that thrive are able to mobilize staff, clarify a sense of purpose, and act as a whole (Heifetz, 1994; Senge, 2011; Wheatley, 2012). A learning-centered college values collaboration and clearly engages leadership and constituents from across the college inclusive of academic and student affairs, administrative services, and information technology units to create a cultural environment committed to increasing the organizational probability that learning will occur.

Second, unless there is an overriding and persistent organizational value of simply engaging in hard work and instilling an organizational comfort level with disequilibrium, there can never be a sustainable commitment to and realization of evidence-based decision making and leadership. The continual loop experience of improving learning systems is an acknowledgment of and willingness to embrace organizational change and discomfort. Living as a learning-centered college is not easy, and it is not simply the maintenance of a status quo experience. Again, contemporary systems thinkers argue repeatedly that hard work and challenging problems bring people and organizations together and that one of the driving purposes of organizations is to solve tough and vexing problems, of which evidence-based decision making, learning outcomes assessment, and continual improvement of student learning are clearly three examples (Senge, 2011; Wheatley, 2012).

Finally, Vickers (1995), a noted pioneer systems thinker, argues that there needs to be an organizational value on "optimizing functional performance . . . seeking to impact on its chosen field" (p. 183). Traditionally, much emphasis has been placed on the metabolic aspects of an organization (including community colleges) such as resource allocation, budgeting, and policies and procedures, but the true measure of the success of an organization should be the degree to which functional performance, in this case learning, is fostered and produced. Functional success can be realized only if there are measurable and recognizable criteria and standards.

In higher education these criteria can be represented by learning and program outcomes, and key performance measures. This functional success as argued by Vickers (1995), then, is "a standard set by the not always unanimous judgment" (p. 183). Not only are there challenges of demonstrating that learning is occurring, but organizational debate as to the most accurate and expedient way to capture the outcomes also continues given the diversity of academic disciplines and levels of faculty engagement. The heart and soul of a community college is to create environments that produce learning—our most important functional outcome (Barr & Tagg, 1995).

The growing accountability movement is demonstrated by such examples as the Voluntary Framework of Accountability (VFA), the first comprehensive accountability system created by community colleges for community colleges (www.aacc.nche.edu/Resources/aaccprograms/VFAWeb/Pages/AboutVFA .aspx); the Completion Agenda, a shared commitment to increasing the number of students with high-quality degrees and certificates by the year 2020 (McPhail, 2011); and performance-based funding. It will, as a result, be the learning-centered culture and the systems within that culture that will foster and ensure student learning and success, ultimately the force that "moves the needle" on the growing number of performance measure indicators. While it is President Obama's Completion Agenda goal of increasing the number of community college graduates by 50% by the year 2020, it is the structure outlined by the American Association of Community Colleges in the VFA that provides the measures for student progress and outcomes, measures for workforce and economic development, and plans for assessment that will demonstrate success.

The foundation of a learning-centered college emerges from the core elements of systems thinking: high levels of organizational interdependence and collaboration, genuine and authentic commitment to hard work and comfort with change, and a clear focus on the functional outcome of learning. It is from these deep-seated cultural underpinnings that the conversation can begin with the topic of visioning.

Visioning

Visions define and declare organizational aspirational directions and future states. Hunt (1998) suggested that a vision serves as an institutional "North Star," always providing that beacon of direction and reminder of what a community college aspires to be. In almost all cases, a vision results in the product of a written statement. Visioning, on the other hand, is more about the process of determining and sustaining the product of that declared vision statement. Visioning is critically important in initializing and establishing a culture of a learning-centered college because it allows for all stakeholders to engage in an organic, iterative, and generative experience that begins to set the cultural foundation, long-term directions, and expected outcomes of the learning-centered college.

How then does one integrate a learning-centered culture as part of the college visioning process? How do organizations move beyond the argument that "we have always been learning centered because, after all, we are institutions of higher learning"? What needs to happen in order for a community college to sustain and continue to grow a culture that values assessment and a commitment to evidence-based decision making and leadership?

In addition to the three underpinning core values mentioned at the beginning of the chapter, a core element from systems thinking is critical to the visioning process. This core element lies in the realization that a learning-centered community college values not only student learning, but also equally employee and organizational learning. It is through the levers of employee and organizational learning that community colleges begin to establish a culture of learning-centeredness. This systems thinking perspective—learning at three levels—fits perfectly with the core community college value and mission of lifelong learning and provides for the starting point for the visioning process. The first key step then is for faculty and staff to begin to learn about being learning-centered professionals. Following are the practical steps that a college can take on this first important step of visioning.

Create Communities of Learners

Develop study groups of college leaders, influencers representing stakeholder groups, and policy group leaders (including union leadership) and provide selected seminal articles and publications that clearly and concisely address concepts and models of a learning-centered college. Provide study guides and compelling questions for discussion and exploration. Writings and publications include "From Teaching to Learning—A New Paradigm for Undergraduate Education" by Barr and Tagg (1995); the joint report of American Association for Higher Education, American College Personnel Association, and NASPA *Powerful Partnerships: A Shared Responsibility for Learning* (1998); and Terry O'Banion's seminal monographs *Creating More Learning-Centered Community Colleges* (1997a) and *A Learning College for the 21st Century* (1997b). More contemporary selections are noted in the references section of this chapter.

Begin the Conversation

Convene learning or strategic conversations in which aspects, characteristics, and the fundamental principles of a learning-centered college are
explored. A variety of facilitation techniques can be used, such as The World
Café, affinity processes, and/or organizational appreciative inquiry. These
conversations will allow faculty and staff to put learning-centered concepts
into the context, history, and existing culture of their own environment. A
powerful way to record these learning experiences is to utilize a professional
"mind mapper" to pictorially through vivid graphic detail tell the story of
faculty and staff's understanding of what a learning-centered college could
look like if realized.

Hold a Big Event

To generate organizational excitement, energy, and inspiration, consider holding a collegewide big event. With the foundational understanding in place
through the community of learners' process, tap into the passion and success
of national thinkers and successful colleagues who have demonstrated, over
time, the transformation into a learning-centered college. Although there is
some risk associated with this—that is, the perception that this is another
"flavor of the month" experience—a big event will begin to crystallize the
transformative movement.

Conduct a Gap Analysis

Explore and discuss incongruent organizational behavior and/or performance gaps between current college practice and the "ideal" learning-
centered environment, elements, and constructs. Define what those gaps
look like. Explore questions such as: Does the language of our current vision,
mission, and values represent and exemplify the elements and characteristics
of a learning-centered college? Do our processes such as strategic planning,
annual budget allocations, personnel selection, and program review reflect
aspects of a learning-centered college? How would major college decisions be
made differently in the context of a learning-centered college? Is evidence-
based decision making and understanding from program review and evaluation at the core of our decision making?

Change the System Language

Collectively craft and/or redraft core mission documents to reflect learning-
centered aspects including your overall vision and mission statement and
core values. See Figures 2.1 and 2.2 for sample vision and core value statements, respectively.

Figure 2.1 Examples of vision statements.

Cuyamaca Community College *promotes learning for the future.*

Ocean County College *aspires to be an institution of distinction where faculty and staff serve to awaken students to a love of learning.*

Doña Ana Community College *will be a premier learning college that is grounded in academic excellence and committed to fostering lifelong learning and active, responsible citizenship within the community.*

Skyline College *inspires a global and diverse community of learners to achieve intellectual, cultural, social, economic, and personal fulfillment.*

Figure 2.2 Examples of core value statements.

Rio Hondo Community College

As a teaching/learning community, we come together and strive to meet the needs, aspirations, and goals of our changing student population and communities.

Cascadia Community College

We stand for a caring community, pluralism & cultural richness, collaboration, access, success, innovation, environmental sustainability, global awareness, responsiveness, creativity.

Lane Community College

Learning: Work together to create a Learning-centered environment; Recognize and respect the unique needs and potential of each learner; Foster a culture of achievement in caring community.

Define and Personalize a Learning-Centered Model

To begin the transformation from conceptual understanding and acceptance to organizational action and behavior, a community college must define and operationalize what a learning-centered college looks like in action. Additionally, it is critically important to personalize and localize concepts and constructs of a learning-centered culture to the unique history and milieu of the existing culture. One way to do this is to develop an institution-specific model that defines the indicators or characteristics of a learning-centered college that fits the needs and culture of the organization. Paradise Valley Community College through this process developed "Indicators of a Learning-Centered College." These indicators were heavily influenced by the work of O'Banion (1999), the Wingspread Group on Higher Education report *An American Imperative: Higher Expectations for Higher Education*

Figure 2.3 Indicators of a learning-centered college.

A Learning-Centered College Ensures That:

1. Learning outcomes that create substantive change in learners are identified and made explicit. These outcomes drive course, program, and curriculum development as well as delivery of student, academic, and administrative support services.
2. Learning outcomes are assessed for the purpose of demonstrating that learning occurred and to expand and improve learning.
3. Learning opportunities are accessible to learners and offered in a variety of formats and options.
4. A culture of student success exists. Student success outcomes emphasize active and engaged learning; a connection with the college environment; goal setting; successful navigation of college processes; and relationship building with faculty, staff, students, and peers. These outcomes are made explicit to students.

Our Systems Support Learning Through:

1. The college's systems (human resources, policies, procedures, structures, technologies, strategic planning, budgeting, and institutional effectiveness processes) and environments being designed and evaluated in terms of their support of learning.
2. Employee and organizational learning programs and the college's employees demonstrating a commitment to continuous learning.
3. Research about learning and learners routinely being considered and systemically incorporated into the college's learning processes, programs, and services. (Indicators, n.d.)

(1993), and ACPA's *The Student Learning Imperative* (1994). Paradise Valley's indicators document allowed the organization to see in concrete terms and actions how a learning-centered college acts on a consistent basis (see Figure 2.3). While the first four indicators focus specifically on the student learning experience, indicators 5–7 focus on the systems that support learning. Critical to the long-term sustainability of a learning-centered culture is the appreciation, expectation, and reward system that values and requires all college units to engage and demonstrate commitment to the learning-centered culture.

Use National Models

Within the community college student learning college movement, a number of colleges, during the visioning process, rather than adopt or create their own principles, have chosen to adopt and operationalize national models and constructs such as the following Learning College Principles as developed by O'Banion (1999):

1. Create substantial change in individual learners.
2. Engage learners in the learning process as full partners assuming primary responsibility for their own learning.
3. Create and offer as many options for learning as possible.
4. Assist learners to form and participate in collaborative learning activities.
5. Define role-learning facilitators by the needs of the learner.
6. Continually assess college programs, policies, and practices to improve the learning environment.

Additionally, it is critical to integrate the core value of learning and elements of a learning-centered college into the strategic planning process, thus fostering organizational decisions and practices that are evidence based.

A number of community colleges have transformed into a learning-centered culture (League for Innovation in the Community College, 1995). One national standard for integrating learning as a core value deeply into the college culture can be seen at Valencia College in Florida, winner of the 2012 Aspen Award for Community College Excellence. Valencia's learning-centered vision, mission, and values are inextricably linked and aligned with the strategic planning, curriculum, budgeting, and student success processes. Valencia's visioning process can be viewed at its website (http://valencia college.edu/lci/plans.cfm). For example, Valencia's Strategic Learning Plan includes a Learning-Centered Reference Guide, What's Learning-Centered About the Budget, and Learning-Centered Core Competencies.

Collaboration

People collaborate when the job they face is too big, is too urgent, or requires too much knowledge for one person or group to do alone. Marshalling what we know about learning and applying it to the education of our students is just such a job. (American Association for Higher Education et al., 1998)

Complementary to O'Banion's Learning College Principles is a set of values and assumptions set forth by the Joint Task Force on Student Learning in *Powerful Partnerships: A Shared Responsibility for Learning* (American Association for Higher Education et al., 1998) including that there be a commitment to view learning holistically, that student and human development are inextricably linked to learning, and that learning encompasses not only the "classroom experience" but cocurricular and experiential opportunities as well. If a college culture embraces these aspects of learning and affirms that learning transcends the traditional Carnegie unit boundary, then authentic and genuine collaboration among all college organizational divisions—not just student and academic affairs, but technology and administrative services as well—is essential for the long-term sustainability of a learning-centered culture.

Given that the delivery of deep student learning experiences transcends artificial organizational hierarchies—in some cases the hierarchy can actually impede student learning and success—the seminal questions to continually pose are: What are the best organizational practices, structures, and processes that encourage, enhance, and support learning? How does an organization promote and reward collaborative leadership? What are the barriers that stifle organizational collaboration? Examples of best practices leading to greater levels of collaboration as well as steps to avoid retrenchment into traditional silos are discussed next.

Ensure Buy-In at the Most Senior Levels

Genuine and authentic buy-in by senior leaders is the most important first step in fostering a collaborative culture. Without a deep level of commitment by senior leaders, it is virtually impossible to live and work collaboratively in a learning-centered college environment. Collaboration at this level, not only "models the way," as argued by Kouzes and Posner (2002), but ensures that the culture will be more than just a series of "loosely coupled" transactions. At this level, vice presidents and deans need to continually and collectively lead within the context of a learning-centered culture when engaging in activities such as strategic planning, financial planning, the annual resource allocation process, and evaluation and assessment, validating the shared outcome and expectation to improve student learning and success.

Colleges transforming into a more collaborative culture need to be prepared to face the following challenges: long and historical organizational boundaries drawn between academic and student affairs; a lack of fully understanding the core values and traditions in the respective functional areas across the college; competition of resources during times of budget retrenchment; failure to clearly articulate the role and direct and indirect relationships of nonacademic areas to student learning; and the need to address the long-held perspective that student affairs, administrative services and other supporting units are "less than" enterprises when mapped against units providing direct teaching and learning experiences.

Building and maintaining a senior-level commitment to collaboration is not a "one and done" handshake. This relationship requires continual attention, support, and nurturing. Mitigation strategies include setting clear expectations that collaboration is an expected part of the leadership culture and that evaluation and reward structures will reflect this expectation when senior-level administrators are hired, continually pushing senior leaders to engage in professional development and readings in broad student learning and success topics that transcend academic and student affairs professional boundaries, and building in opportunities for shared leadership for core college programs and initiatives directly related to the core processes supporting student learning and success.

Use Professional Development Opportunities to Build Collaboration at the System Level

Professional development opportunities that target student learning, learning outcomes assessment, and evidence-based decision making need to be made universally available to faculty and staff inclusive of college divisions. These types of experiences are not just for the academic and student affairs domains. It is imperative that, for example, the facilities department knows how campus ecology and purposefully designed common spaces can make a significant contribution to student learning and success. Or that information technology leadership has the core knowledge to partner with academic and student affairs to develop and implement technology tools that promote student success. A learning-centered culture will thrive most when done in a culture that values not only student learning, but also employee and organizational learning. The provision of these learning opportunities to all employees and the leadership expectation of participation of all employees send a strong message that there is an organizational vested interest in the need to continually develop skills and practices that support student learning and success. Without this common knowledge, it is nearly impossible to garner meaningful collaboration around programs, activities, and services that produce and support student learning and success.

Use Assessment as a Collaborative Process

Given that the assessment of student learning outcomes (SLOs) and program review are key elements of a learning-centered college, the development and execution of the assessment process can serve as a key collaborative rallying point. Evaluation and assessment tools used in student and academic affairs can share elements that support student learning and measures of SLOs. The expectation that outcomes assessment is required and viewed as a critical systemic aspect of the institution creates allies and enablers among academic and student affairs, administrative services, and information technology professionals. The assessment of SLOs, when valued for both faculty and "out-of-class" professionals, can create assessment communities within the institution. The challenges associated with assessment (i.e., high levels of engagement and participation, translation of general education rubrics across the curriculum and cocurriculum, allocation of time for the analysis and use of assessment findings) provide a sense of "we are all in this together," and an opportunity to leverage a divisional interdependency and sharing of limited support resources to accomplish the task at hand.

Integrate Committees That Oversee In- and Out-of-Class Assessment of Student Learning

While many colleges maintain both an academic assessment team and an out-of-class assessment team, the addition of an oversight assessment group that aligns, monitors, and maintains institution-wide assessment activities furthers the collaborative culture. Often, powerful synergies can arise out of these partnership opportunities. For example, at Paradise Valley Community College, the general education rubrics for problem solving, oral communication, and information literacy are commonly used in the out-of-class environment in student affairs programs. Aggregated findings from the out-of-class use are included in the college's annual assessment reports in order to provide a more complete assessment of student learning.

Consider Joint and Co-Leadership Appointments

The use of joint and/or co-appointments to lead programs that "straddle" the traditional student and academic affairs hierarchical structures can also be an effective strategy to embed collaboration (Schroeder, 1999). Student development and learning is not naturally contained in artificial silos of academic and student affairs organizational structures. There are a number of programs that contain equally robust academic and student affairs roles and functions, including learning communities; First-Year Experience; early access high school bridge programs (e.g., early college, dual enrollment, concurrent enrollment); and career services that include credit experiences such as internships and cooperative work experiences, service-learning with curricular-based learning outcomes as part of volunteer learning experiences, and civic engagement programming. Although there are challenges with programs with direct or dotted-line reports to two divisions, these programs can also serve as a linking function to develop greater organizational collaboration.

Leverage Funding to Encourage Collaboration

With limited availably of new funding and, in some cases, the necessity of reallocating existing base budget funding, the use of any funding mechanism to support innovation initiatives and pilot programs can also be a lever for organizational collaboration. Multi- or cross-departmental sponsorship and engagement can be made an expectation for funding. Additionally, the organizational processes in place to evaluate the implementation of new programs or services can also require that the collaborative delivery of services serve as a criterion for new program implementation.

Challenge the Traditional Organizational Hierarchy and Structure

A number of community colleges have joined a national trend to merge academic and student affairs under the leadership of a single vice president. Organizational synergies, such as greater integration of faculty in the out-of-class programming, ease of communication and sharing of resources, and more effective integration of assessment practices, can be achieved through aligning reporting relationships among functions traditionally labeled as student or academic support services—programs that directly or indirectly support classroom learning. The integration of student development and success strategies and practices, typically in the professional domain of student affairs, with academic support services such as learning support centers, computer commons, honors centers, and student success courses can be an effective outcome of the merger. Community colleges such as Scottsdale Community College, Lane Community College, Tacoma Community College, and Finger Lakes Community College have implemented this collaborative organizational structure.

Embed Faculty Within Student Affairs Programs

One alternative to a more radical organization redesign to enhance a culture of collaboration is to aggressively and purposely embed faculty into traditional student affairs programs and services. Faculty can serve in roles such as mentors, success coaches, and/or club advisers. For example, at Paradise Valley Community College, each intercollegiate athletic team is assigned a faculty member (compensated as overload) team liaison. In this role, the faculty member is engaged in the following activities: participating in the early alert process and thus in the intervention with student-athletes falling behind in academic course work, meeting with the athletic teams in concert with the coaches to stress academic expectations, and meeting individually with student-athletes to address academic and career issues. Another way that faculty can provide collaborative support for a student development program is to install co-leadership with a student affairs professional for minority male empowerment programs. Faculty leadership adds credibility to the program with peer faculty as well as provides a student learning focus in conjunction with the student support and development programming.

Communication

Perhaps one of the most understated roles of the college president and senior college leadership is to keep the college "on message" as an institution deeply committed to and passionate about student learning and success. As the presidential leadership moves further toward fund-raising and community relations, it remains important that the role continue as a champion for student learning and success. The task, then, is to embed this message as part of the college culture so that it becomes a natural part of all dialogue, not in a forced or artificial manner, but one with genuine application and meaning. Although this sounds simple, as leadership engages in the maintenance, operation, and delivery of core college systems, it is amazing how quickly the focus can become, as Vickers (1995) suggests, on the metabolic aspects (keeping the organization running and moving forward) rather than on the functional outcomes of student learning and success. Visual, written, and behavioral messages are levers to implement, develop, grow, and sustain the learning-centered culture. Members of an organization pay attention to what is clearly, consistently, and passionately talked and written about.

Learning-Centered Messaging

Learning-centered messaging will permeate deep into the organization, as it is included in all major college communication processes and strategies. One tactic is to establish learning-centered or learning college websites. For example, Estrella Mountain Community College, Aims Community College, Cascadia Community College, and Paradise Valley Community College have established learning college home pages. Information on these pages includes a message from the college's president; definitions of the characteristics of learning-centered colleges; links to assessment and strategic planning pages; and testimonies from faculty, staff, and students on the impact of learning and working in a learning-centered college. The web pages serve as a resource for employee learning about learning-centered practices, a repository for college learning-centered artifacts, and a means to chronicle and document continued progress in the learning-centered journey.

Additional strategies to embed learning-centered language in the institutional messaging process include the following:

- Adopt a college motto or tagline that reflects the notion of a learning-centered college. For example, the Paradise Valley Community College motto is "The Power of Learning." Aims Community College adopted the slogan "We're all about students. Your dream is our mission."
- Utilize an annual theme that includes powerful words that connect to the vision of student learning and success.
- Make visible language related to student learning, assessment of SLOs, and effective teaching and learning practices in primary college documents beyond the mission, vision, and value statements including

strategic planning documents, diversity and inclusion plans, facilities master plans, and long-term financial plans.

- Consider including a college's motto, learning tagline, or complementary logo in images and visuals used by the college such as PowerPoint presentations, footers on printed materials, or signs on campus.

Language and Individual Messaging

Learning-centered language varies among colleges that have adopted learning-centered practices, and it is critical that faculty and staff understand the meaning behind the language. For example, colleges may use the term *learning-centered* or *learner-centered* or *student-centered*. There is also variation in broader terms of a learning-centered college versus a learning college. Regardless of the language selected, it is paramount that definitions be made clear and used consistently across the college.

College presidents have a number of opportunities to reinforce the institution's commitment to learning-centered practices on a regular basis. Through their monthly or quarterly internal communication pieces, presidents can reference and highlight outstanding examples of learning-centered practices. For example, the president at South Mountain Community College includes learning links to online written and/or video resources that address learning-centered practices as part of the weekly presidential update. Estrella Mountain Community College publishes The Learning College Yearbook, which highlights activities that capture the essence of learning (see www.estrellamountain.edu/sites/all/themes/emcc/images/learning-college/emcc-lc-yearbook-web.pdf). Other opportunities to communicate a college's commitment to learning-centered practices include a presidential welcome greeting on websites, as well as welcomes in student handbooks and college catalogs and publications shared with external advisory groups.

Messaging to Students

Similar to the opportunities to communicate learning-centered messages to employees, many of the same opportunities are available for use with students. Ironically—given that student learning is a primary focus of a learning-centered college—opportunities to communicate to students are often missed or overlooked. Although students are not necessarily interested in the organizational structure of a learning-centered culture, it is important to communicate manifestations of the learning experience such as effective learning strategies and practices, student success skills and behaviors, engagement and involvement strategies, and the challenge and expectation of deep versus surface learning. If we do not tell students how to be successful, then how can we expect them to know how to be active and engaged in the process?

Direct information and expectations about the learning assessment processes through course syllabi is also a critical communication strategy.

Telling Stories

Goodman (2003) argues that the single most powerful communication method is storytelling and that within as short as 60 seconds, a powerful story can be told that includes the protagonist, the barrier-laden pursuit of goals, and the final resolution. He skillfully argues that higher education attempts to tell our story through bar graphs, charts, and narrative heavily laden with higher education jargon (Council for Advancement and Support of Education, 2012). When one looks at the elements of telling a story, it is clear that in many cases this is just how the learning process unfolds in the community college. The protagonists in this "community college story" are from diverse backgrounds and include students from historically underrepresented backgrounds, first-generation students, working adult students, and underprepared students. The barriers are also abundant: interference from multiple life roles, extended length of time in pursuit of a degree because of the need to complete developmental courses, and the need to develop the skills required to learn effectively. Finally, it is the realization of moments of learning instances that brings students one step closer to their goals of certificate or degree completion, transfer to a four-year college or university, or entrance into the workforce. It is these real-life student stories that can best describe what a learning-centered college looks and feels like. Although aggregated average rubric scores and narrative summaries of how learning is being improved from collegewide annual general assessment reports demonstrate the evidence, it is the student success stories that bring learning-centeredness alive. Many powerful examples of student stories are posted on YouTube, including stories from Community College of Rhode Island's Class of 2012, Ivy Tech Community College, Central Piedmont Community College, North Platte Community College, and Bristol Community College.

Garnering Sustained Buy-In

The discussion thus far has focused on the elements that launch and maintain the culture during the initial stages of development leading to a "more" learning-centered college environment. The importance of visioning, organizational collaboration, and communication has been addressed. It is through these processes that organizational systems such as strategic planning, budget and resource allocation, and evaluation and assessment processes become the structural foundations in which the learning-centered culture can grow. But over time, with faculty and staff turnover, budgetary reductions, and the rapidly changing world of technology and technology-supported learning strategies, how does an organization sustain and more deeply embed the learning-centered culture in the community college environment?

This final discussion of garnering support to sustain a learning-centered college culture rests on the not-so-obvious assumption that a learning-centered culture is truly and noticeably different and produces different types of results than does a college whose values and organizational behavior are not as deeply oriented as those of a learning-centered college. In essence, a college's task is to look continually at how it has defined its "learning-centeredness"—through its own homegrown model or the adoption of a national model—and to continually ask these questions: Are we still living these principles? Does the relentless pursuit of increasing student learning still dominate organizational conversations and agendas? Is significant time being spent on understanding and using data and information from our assessment and evaluation commitments?

Practical strategies for sustaining and garnering long-term buy-in of a learning-centered culture must be focused on two fronts: (a) organizational structures and (b) the continual professional development and orientation of a college core of faculty and staff experiencing normal attrition.

Sustaining the Organization

Implementing strategies to sustain and perpetuate the learner-centered focus over time is necessary in order to ensure such a focus becomes a viable part of an organization's culture and does not fizzle out due to lack of priority, interest, or resources. The following strategies offer a number of practical ways to support the creation of a strong learner-centered culture on a community and two-year college campus.

Develop an Annual Internal Learning-Centered College Report Card

Learning-centered colleges will have developed and implemented a model or adopted a set of markers or indicators that define their learning-centeredness. A quick and easy way to take an annual pulse of the college's continued commitment to learning-centered practices is simply to gather evidence of organizational practice and behavior aligned against the institutional indicators. The outcome is a public statement that describes the progress, programs, and artifacts that support the realization of learning-centered practices. For example, if one of the college's indicators is "Learning opportunities are accessible to learners and offered in a variety of formats and options," the learning-centered report card might then list specific examples of how this indicator was actualized throughout the year with evidence such as changes in frequency of course-type offerings, types of professional development offered to support new and innovative formats, student satisfaction and success rates in nontraditional course formats, and resources committed to the support of alternative delivery methods.

Review the College's Major Planning Systems and Processes

As significant processes such as strategic planning, annual budget allocations, facilities planning, technology coordination and planning are operational-ized, the need remains, on an annual basis, to gather evidence of continued alignment and connection to the core value of learning-centeredness. As processes are updated (e.g., program review or the assessment of student learning out of class) can enhancements be made to further align practice with the core learning-centered values? It is important that as new faculty and staff are added to these teams and committees, time be spent on renewing the commitment that the mission and charge of the teams are central to the learning-centered outcomes and practices.

Live the Culture

As the learning-centered culture grows and colleges adopt mottos, taglines, icons, and celebrations of learning, ensure that these artifacts continue to be a part of college meetings, convocations, and published annual reports. As learning-centered colleges mature, typically less time is spent talking about the organization and indicators and more on the manifestations such as learning outcomes assessment results, success stories of deep student learn-ing and success, and celebrations around meeting and exceeding performance measures. Living the culture requires the organizational ability to communicate the results of the culture and less of the mechanics of learning-centeredness.

Sustaining the People in the Organization

Ultimately it is all about people and relationships: Garnering buy-in and long-term support of the learning-centered culture requires a significant organizational investment in the human resources of the organization. In a community college environment there is significant turnover on the front lines, in many cases staffed by part-time and temporary staff. Additionally, as the older baby boomers begin to retire, there will be significant turnover in the veteran faculty and leadership ranks. Thus, there is a strong need to continue with employee and organizational learning on a sustained basis.

Cultivate New Champions

In many cases, the "movement" to become a learning-centered college begins with an impassioned college president or vice president. Unless this leader-ship passion is pushed into the organization and new leaders gain an equal footing and confidence in communicating the message and translating concept into practice, the movement will fade away. All of the senior leaders must be skilled in articulating the learning-centered messages both in the context of their respective functional areas and at the system level. It is not enough for leaders to have a learning-centered college "elevator speech"; long-term champions must lead and communicate with conviction and deep understanding. New champions can be cultivated through learning-centered topical programming such as learning-centered practices, assessment and evaluation in a learning-centered college, and learning-centered practices in student and administrative services.

Integrate Learning-Centeredness Into the Hiring Process

A clear indication that an organization is committed to a learning-centered culture is the inclusion of requirements and expectations in the minimum and desired job-posting qualifications as new faculty and leadership positions are filled. Additionally, an organization should provide all prospective applicants with information resources that explain the college's commitment to learning-centered practices, and the organization should require that faculty candidates have demonstrated experience in and commitment to learning outcomes assessment, student engagement strategies, and other learning-centered practices. Further, hiring expectations for leaders should include demonstrated experience in evidence-based decision making, and the screening rubrics and interview processes should be shaped so that learning-centered experiences play a significant role in the hiring decisions.

Leverage the New Employee Onboarding Process

Before new faculty and staff arrive, they should be provided with welcome letters that include copies of college reports or learning-centered primers to reinforce the commitment to learning-centered practices. New faculty and staff orientations must include a learning-centered "academy" in which significant time is spent in conversation about the role of the employee in actualizing learning-centered practices. At Paradise Valley Community College, Learning-Centered Guides for both faculty and staff have been developed. These guides pose reflective statements that allow new employees to explore and understand how the role and expectations in a learning-centered college are different:

1. I have a personal definition of learning (with a conceptual/theoretical basis or a practical concrete explanation).
2. I can describe with concrete examples how my daily work at the college contributes to student learning.
3. I can give a genuine, authentic, two-minute "elevator speech" on why learning is our core value and what being learning-centered means.

4. My division/departments utilize the Seven Indicators of a Learning-Centered College as a basis for practice and discusses the indicators on a regular basis.

5. Assessment of student learning is part of the practice of my department or division.

6. I understand and can explain how the following student success factors are connected to student learning: relationship building with faculty, staff, and other students; setting of educational and career goals; actively engaging in educationally purposeful activities (including active learning strategies); and developing a sense of connectedness and belonging with the college.

7. I learn about learning on a regular basis (e.g., read current literature, attend sessions on learning, etc.). (Paradise Valley Community College, 2013).

Make Leadership Accountable

Senior administrative and faculty leadership need to have aspects of leading in a learning-centered college as part of their ongoing evaluation and professional development plans. Per these plans, the leaders would lead units that consistently achieve exemplary assessment and program review results, demonstrate effective and efficient resource allocation tied to evidence-based decision making, and sustain innovative learning-centered practices.

Conclusion

The task of establishing and maintaining a learning-centered culture requires significant commitment to organizational leadership. A core value in a learning-centered college, evidence-based decision making, enhances organizational practice and improves levels of student success and learning. This cycle of improvement requires constant attention to the attributes and indicators of learning-centered practices. The focus of this attention lies in the core systems thinking, the organizational values of focus on the functional outcomes of student learning and success, a commitment to hard work and complex organizational problem solving, and a deeply embedded collaborative culture.

References

American Association for Higher Education, American College Personnel Association, and NASPA: Student Affairs Administrators in Higher Education. (1998). *Powerful partnerships: A shared responsibility for learning*. Retrieved from http://www.naspa.org/career/sharedresp.cfm

American College Personnel Association. (1994). *The student learning imperative: Implications for student affairs*. Washington, DC: Author.

Barr, R. B., & Tagg, J. (1995). From teaching to learning—a new paradigm for undergraduate education. *Change, 27*(6), 12–25.

Council for Advancement and Support of Education. (2012, October 10). Be a better storyteller for your college. *Community College Advancement News, 2*(4). Retrieved from http://www.case.org/Publications_and_Products/October2012/Be_a_Better_Storyteller_for_Your_College.html

Dewey, J. (1927). *The public and its problems.* New York, NY: Holt.

Goodman, A. (2003). *Storytelling as best practice.* Retrieved from http://www.agoodmanonline.com/publications/storytelling/index.html

Heifetz, R. (1994). *Leadership without easy answers.* Cambridge, MA: The Belknap Press of Harvard University Press.

Hunt, M. (1998). *Dream makers putting vision and values to work.* Palo Alto, CA: Davies-Black.

Indicators of a LCC. (n.d.). In *Paradise Valley Community College: Learning centered college.* Retrieved from http:// www.pvc.maricopa.edu/learning-centered/indicators-lcc

Kouzes, J. M., & Posner, B. Z. (2002). *The leadership challenge.* San Francisco, CA: Jossey-Bass.

League for Innovation in the Community College. (1995). Learning College Project Vanguard Colleges. Retrieved from http://www.league.org/league/projects/lcp/vanguard.htm

McPhail, C. J. (2011). *The completion agenda: A call to action.* Summary report from the November 10–11, 2010, meeting of the American Association of Community Colleges Commissions and Board of Directors. Retrieved from http://www.aacc.nche.edu/Publications/Reports/Documents/CompletionAgenda_report.pdf

O'Banion, T. (1997a). *Creating more learning-centered community colleges.* Washington, DC: American Association of Community Colleges and American Council on Education Series on Higher Education, Oryx Press.

O'Banion, T. (1997b). *A learning college for the 21st century.* Washington, DC: American Association of Community Colleges and American Council on Education Series on Higher Education, Oryx Press.

O'Banion, T. (1999). *Launching a learning-centered college.* Chandler, AZ: League for Innovation in the Community College.

Paradise Valley Community College. (2013). *Learning Centered Guides.* (unpublished professional development handout). Author: Phoenix, AZ.

Schroeder, C. (1999). Partnerships: An imperative for enhancing student learning and institutional effectiveness. *New Directions for Student Services, 1999*(87), 5–18.

Senge, P. (2011). *Navigating Webs of interdependence* [Video]. http://www.youtube.com/watch?v=HOPfVVMCwYg

Vickers, Sir G. (1995). *The art of judgment: A study of policy making.* Thousand Oaks, CA: SAGE.

Wheatley, M. (2012). *Let go & lead: Meg Wheatley on solving tough problems* [Video]. http://www.youtube.com/watch?v=ef7lmOUnaik&playnext=1&list =PL421FAFCF8C85096F&feature=results_video

Wingspread Group on Higher Education. (1993). *An American imperative: Higher expectations for higher education.* Racine, WI: Author.

Storytelling Examples

BCC Student Success Stories—Ashley Tillman, Bristol Community College (www.youtube.com/watch?v=zrvqyP0ba9g)
CPCC Learning Centered, Central Piedmont Community College (www.youtube.com/watch?v=lMCgTZmonnc)
Community College, A Personal Story: Alicia Baldwin, Ivy Tech Community College (www.youtube.com/watch?v=xR7A4Q9jihk)
Student Success at North Platte Community College, North Platte Community College (www.youtube.com/watch?v=H28q96YhKWc)
Student Success Stories: Commencement 2012, Members of the Community College of Rhode Island's Class of 2012 (www.youtube.com/watch?v= n3VMFpRR4IE)

Community College Learning-Centered Websites

Aims Community College (www.aims.edu/about/learningCollege/)
Cascadia Community College (www.cascadia.edu/discover/about/teaching/default.aspx)
Estrella Mountain Community College (www.estrellamountain.edu/learning -college)
Paradise Valley Community College (www.pvc.maricopa.edu/learning -centered/presidents-message)

3

DEVELOPING SHARED LEARNING OUTCOMES AND DETERMINING PRIORITIES FOR ASSESSMENT

Barbara June Rodriguez and John Frederick

The traditional concept of a community or two-year college includes an institution with an open-access policy that confers associate degrees and certificates. Such institutions provide students with the appropriate skills to enter the workforce immediately or transfer to a senior institution with an associate's degree. As a result of their missions, community and two-year colleges are poised to address the calls for accountability from external constituents (Banta, Black, Kahn, & Jackson, 2004). A primary expectation of accountability is the assessment of student learning outcomes (SLOs). Learning outcomes describe the students' intended educational attainment in terms of specific knowledge, skills, and attitudes (Maki, 2004; Suskie, 2009; Walvoord, 2010).

Developing an effective learning outcomes statement is akin to writing a simple sentence with a direct object; it contains a subject, a verb, and an object. A learning outcome focuses on the action performed by the student; thus, the student is the subject. Next, the appropriate selection of a verb for the learning outcome is essential. Because a learning outcomes statement measures knowledge, skills, and attitudes, applying Bloom's Taxonomy (1956) to select the verb is a common approach (Palomba & Banta, 1999; Suskie, 2009). Bloom's Taxonomy consists of three domains: cognitive, psychomotor, and affective; therefore, the outcome can be written to measure its intent. In the same grammatical context that a direct object receives the action of the verb or is a result of the action, so is the object in a learning outcomes statement.

For example, in the learning outcomes statement *The student will design an analog electrical circuit,* the circuit is the object because the student (subject) will design (verb) the electrical circuit (direct object). Once the foundational knowledge exists to develop learning outcomes statements, this information can be applied at various levels within an institution.

Moreover, because 45 states and the District of Columbia have adopted the Common Core State Standards (CCSS), community and two-year colleges may wish to consider using Norman Webb's (1997) Depth of Knowledge (DOK) in conjunction with Bloom's Taxonomy. We make this proposal because the CCSS seeks both to define what K–12 students need to be able to demonstrate they have achieved proficiency and to show they are prepared to enter college programs or the workforce (National Governors Association Center for Best Practices, Council of Chief State School Officers, 2010). Webb's DOK is a four-level scale that focuses on the cognitive demand of the assessment measure and looks beyond the verb selected in the outcome. Therefore, institutions that become familiar with DOK will have a better understanding of the twenty-first-century student's learning framework. Incorporating DOK into assessment conversations at community and two-year colleges provides an additional mechanism for institutions to evaluate assessment measures to ensure that they are designed to elicit the expected performance standard.

In the context of SLOs and assessment at a community or two-year college, SLOs are usually established on three levels: course, program, and institutional. Generally, the institutional-level learning outcomes are also known as the general education outcomes. General education refers to the courses that are required by all students to obtain the degree. The program level encompasses student services departments, and these outcomes are often characterized as cocurricular activities. These *activities* are defined as formal and informal out-of-class learning opportunities.

In the community and two-year college environment, a question that comes up year after year and conference after conference is: What should be developed first, course-level outcomes, program learning outcomes, or general education learning outcomes? The answer to that question rests solely on the existing culture of the institution. Establishing shared learning outcomes is a collaborative process that "has no universal model that fits all institutions. Rather, individual institutions embed or evolve practices that enable them to sustain a culture of inquiry" (Maki, 2004, p. 4). This chapter provides strategies for building shared learning outcomes, reflects on potential structures within the institution that can be utilized to support the various assessment initiatives, identifies strategies for engaging faculty and student services in the assessment initiatives, and determines priorities for assessment.

Strategies for Building Shared Learning Outcomes

According to Hutchings (2011), "In the last decade, some form of assessment has been required as part of the institutional accreditation process, so most campuses today have at least some assessment activity underway" (p. 2). Unfortunately, a significant amount of these assessment activities are not components of an institutional systematic process; instead, assessment occurs in silos and at varying levels of sophistication and effectiveness. Some institutions feel pressured and, as a result, rush to make sure they document that assessment has occurred prior to their reaccreditation visit. Realistically, this approach is not conducive to establishing a culture of assessment and inquiry, but it happens often. A sustainable assessment model should not be rushed. Even with a rocky beginning, community and two-year college administrations can employ specific strategies to "hit the reset button" on assessment. Developing a comprehensive assessment process with input from all stakeholders—faculty, students, staff, and administrators—is the foundation for building shared learning outcomes. Elements of this foundation include an emphasis on quality instruction and student learning articulated in the college's mission, vision, and values; professional development and training; and incorporation of SLOs and assessment within the college's strategic plan to ensure an adequate level of budgetary resources.

Mission, Vision, and Values

The institutional mission sets the tone and expectations for the internal and external constituents. An institution may not have identified a mission, a vision, and values as components of its ongoing planning and evaluation process, but generally two of the three components exist; if not, this omission needs to be addressed. Through the process of developing a shared mission, vision, and/or values, the stakeholders have the opportunity to collaborate on what the collective group believes is the institution's purpose. The quality of instruction and learning will therefore naturally become a shared investment and priority for the stakeholders. The wonderful aspect of an institution's mission is that it can change as a result of its environment. Community and two-year colleges thus need to engage in a self-assessment, and if the importance of quality teaching and learning as demonstrated through assessing student learning is not evident in the mission, vision, and values, this should be seen as an opportunity for the institution to start the conversation and set the tone for building shared learning outcomes.

Professional Development and Training

A common theme pervasive in the literature and research is that effective assessment requires faculty and administrator buy-in and that assessment should be faculty driven (Angelo, 2002; Díaz-Lefebvre, 2003; Hutchings,

2010). Similar to assessment in the cocurricular environment, for faculty to be in the driver's seat, professional development and training is paramount. Through training, faculty can connect the learning that occurs in the classroom to the learning they expect within their programs while naturally aligning the course- and program-level outcomes with the institutional-level learning outcomes. Too often faculty and student services professionals are expected to develop and assess SLOs without the training, which is counterproductive. Moreover, a combination of a sense of urgency and inadequate resources and professionals to provide the training compounds an already difficult situation. Through training, faculty and student service professionals learn assessment terminology and are able to apply these terms in the context of their professional responsibilities. The training also provides the environment to explain the levels of learning outcomes and how they affect one another. Because of budgetary restrictions, professional development and training is one of the first areas to receive less funding, but if the professional development and training is effectively organized and well thought out, it can be successful. As in so many community and two-year colleges, professional development is handled by a committee of faculty and staff members under the category of "other duties as assigned," or the professional and training department consists of one to three professionals who have more than student learning and assessment on which to focus.

Curriculum Mapping

Developing various types of curriculum maps or matrices for the various academic and student services divisions is an excellent strategy for building shared learning outcomes. A common definition used for *curriculum mapping* is a "method to align instruction with desired goals and program outcomes. It can also be used to explore what is taught and how" (University of Hawai'i at Mānoa). Curriculum mapping is beneficial for the institution regardless of the order in which it develops its levels of learning outcomes—course, program, or institutional (general education). Learning starts in the classroom, so it is a great place to start the curriculum-mapping process, which in turn helps the institution build shared learning outcomes. If the college does not have written learning outcomes for each of its courses, then faculty must develop the outcomes. Course-level learning outcomes are the catalyst for program- and institutional-level learning outcomes. In terms of curriculum mapping, the general concept is for academic affairs and student services divisions to frame discussions around this question: What do we want our students to learn? The college's organizational structure and culture determine the number of discussions and the format. The result of these discussions is a list of abilities, knowledge, values, and/or attitudes. The list is prioritized and becomes the program-level learning outcomes. Through this integrated process, the institution engages the college's stakeholders, resulting in a master curriculum map that serves as tangible evidence of shared learning outcomes.

Institutional Structures Supporting Assessment Initiatives

For assessment initiatives to be effective and ongoing, multidimensional levels of institutional support are essential; these supporting structures include the strategic plan, the administration, and a systematic assessment process. The college administration should evaluate the existing strategic plan and assessment process to ascertain the value; if improvements are needed, the administration in collaboration with faculty and staff serves as the catalyst for change.

Strategic Plan

A strategic plan is the most important institutional structure that needs to be in place to support the assessment initiative. The strategic plan encompasses the institution's mission, vision, and values. Through the strategic plan, the college articulates its direction and priorities. Incorporating assessment initiatives within the strategic plan demonstrates a commitment to high-quality education and student learning. This commitment also requires allocating the necessary resources; therefore, the inclusion of assessment in the strategic plan indicates that some degree of resources will be available.

Administration

Initiative may be defined as the ability to begin or to follow through energetically with a plan. An assessment initiative without a supportive administration is not really an assessment initiative. Although it is true that assessment is often faculty driven, it should be a partnership with administration and student services. More often than not, the student services division is marginalized when it comes to being engaged in the assessment of student learning because there is a misconception that student learning is only about a student's classroom experience. Even in a commuter environment, students regularly interact with college departments outside of the classroom, such as advisement, student life, and financial aid. Therefore, the student services division should be engaged from the beginning, and this is the administration's responsibility.

The college president sets the tone for the assessment initiative, so when one thinks about the conceptual framework that would ensure an institutional structure that successfully supports assessment, John Kotter's (1996)

Leading Change should come to mind. The college president and the college's board of trustees have business leadership models to practice that coincide with the needs of establishing and supporting an assessment initiative. According to Kotter, there are eight stages of change:

1. Establish a sense of urgency.
2. Create a guiding coalition.
3. Create a change vision.
4. Communicate the vision for buy-in.
5. Empower broad-based action.
6. Plan for and create short-term wins.
7. Never let up.
8. Incorporate change into the culture.

Even if the connection is unintentional, there is a connection between these stages and an institution's support of an assessment initiative. To highlight some of the similarities between Kotter's stages of change and an institution's assessment initiative, a college's sense of urgency usually comes from a looming reaffirmation from one of the seven regional accrediting organizations recognized by the U.S. Department of Education, but the sense of urgency mounts with college completion initiatives and the decline in funding from states. To develop and sustain the assessment initiative a team of committed and respected faculty, student services professionals, and administrators needs to be assembled to lead the assessment initiative. Through this assessment alliance, a shared purpose is created, along with strategies to achieve the purpose.

Assessment Process

Too often community and two-year college professionals start the assessment initiative without a clear process in place, which is a primary reason why assessment fails. The components and expectations of an institutional assessment process should be clearly articulated in writing and available to all college stakeholders. This process should include definitions of assessment terms; curriculum mapping; assessment templates to report learning outcome statements, direct and indirect measures, standards, and results; and timelines and steps for assessment development and implementation. Ideally, the college will also develop an assessment resource manual for future direction and reference.

Strategies to Engage Faculty and Student Services

To avoid assessment becoming stagnant, faculty and student services professionals need to be continually engaged and energized about outcomes-based assessment. Making assessment consistently prevalent requires stakeholders to appreciate its relevancy and to feel valued through a variety of incentives.

Relevancy

The same type of philosophy that applies to engaging students in the classroom applies to engaging faculty and student services in assessment. Just as students need to know the relevancy of the knowledge and skills they gain through the learning process, faculty and student services professionals need to know the relevancy and significance of assessment to teaching and learning. Hutchings (2010) proposed recommendations to engage faculty, some of which reinforce the importance of making assessment relevant, such as building assessment around the regular, ongoing work of teaching and learning and incorporating topics related to teaching and learning in regularly scheduled departmental meetings. Colleges should foster an environment where assessment is an integral part of the teaching and learning process. If academic and student services departments are introduced to assessment by being asked questions to which they can relate, establishing shared outcomes becomes much simpler and sustainable. Based on the work of Palomba and Banta (1999), Schuh and Upcraft (2001), and Suskie (2009), we believe that these are some of the questions to ask: What is our program or department trying to accomplish? How well are we doing it? How can we improve what we are currently doing? How can student learning be improved? Although basic, these questions encompass the essential elements of assessment without using the word *assessment*. Sometimes, to garner buy-in the word *assessment* may need to be avoided until college stakeholders start to embrace the importance of the concepts of assessment. Once this takes place, the word can be used more freely. Moreover, colleges need to self-reflect on their meeting agendas to gauge how often teaching and learning is an agenda item. If teaching and learning becomes important only when it is time for reaccreditation, colleges will struggle with establishing shared learning outcomes. Faculty and student services professionals enjoy talking about the impact they make on students' lives and successes, so incorporating these conversations into departmental meetings is paramount for engagement. Meetings should move beyond the traditional focus of operational minutiae and incorporate teaching and learning.

Incentives

Traditionally in a community or two-year college environment, the use of incentives as a strategy for engagement is generally designed for faculty, not student services professionals. However, based on a study by Kezar (2001), an institution should "question the culture of student affairs that could downplay the importance of incentives" (p. 50). Therefore, community colleges should consider student services professionals as well as faculty when making decisions about incentives. Some colleges provide stipends and course-load reductions for faculty who serve on assessment committees or participate in the assessment process. Stipends can be offered for student services professionals as well. To ensure a shared and collaborative assessment process, student services professionals can play an integral role in assessment committees. Whereas some institutions would like to offer stipends or hire additional adjunct faculty but cannot afford to, there are others that prefer not to use monetary compensation as an incentive. When these factors apply, an institution may have a system in place or should create a structure to acknowledge faculty and student services professionals through awards; certificates; or affirming gestures, such as providing lunch and refreshments during committee meetings. Faculty and staff generally understand the financial limitations of an institution; therefore, no matter how small, consistent tokens of appreciation and support can go a long way in engaging faculty and student services professionals in the assessment process.

Thinking About Activity

An effective, collaborative activity that can include both academic affairs and student services divisions is applying the SWOT analysis to the college's learning outcomes assessment initiative. A SWOT analysis evaluates the strengths, weaknesses, opportunities, and threats of a project or an organization. This analysis helps in the planning process and supports shared ownership of the initiative. Generally speaking, strengths and weaknesses are internal factors whereas opportunities and threats are external factors.

Complete a SWOT analysis on the existing structure at your institution in relation to its learning outcomes assessment processes. Then answer these questions: What did you find most interesting? What strategies do you have to overcome the weaknesses and threats? What strategies do you recommend to capitalize on your institution's strengths and opportunities?

Once the institution has established its shared learning outcomes, it is important for the institution to prioritize assessment of those learning outcomes. Setting priorities for assessment may be easier said than done because of the institutional culture and attitudes toward assessment, as well as internal and external factors that affect assessment priorities. An internal faculty and student services–driven attitude of "assessment matters" because it focuses on improvement of learning and teaching can aid in the setting of priorities. Other internal factors such as the mission of the institution, previous assessment data and results or lack thereof, and institutional budgets may dictate assessment priorities. While internal factors present their unique set of challenges, the need to be accountable to external stakeholders such as accrediting organizations and employers (national or regional, or specialized accrediting agencies) presents another set of challenges. Finally, the community that the institution primarily serves has a vested interest in the student learning.

Why Assessment Should Be a Priority

Assessment should be a priority because assessment matters. According to Suskie (2009), "Colleges and universities increasingly are emphasizing the assessment of student learning for two primary reasons: improvement and accountability" (p. 58). If the purpose of assessment is improvement, then there is an intentional focus on the improvement of student learning and achievement, teaching, and data-driven decision making. If, however, the purpose of assessment is accountability, then the focus is on proving to external stakeholders the efficacy of one's assessment processes, program quality, and institution. While both foci are important, each purpose has its own strengths and limitations.

Some strengths of focusing on improvement are better decision making based on data that positively impact student learning, the curriculum, faculty and staff professional development, and efficient allocation of funds and resources to support student learning endeavors. Similarly, a focus on accountability can lead to more informed institutional decision making for planning, allocation of funds and resources, improvement to the assessment process, a systematic documentation of processes, greater transparency, and culpability to internal and external stakeholders. Ironically, the strengths of assessment for improvement and accountability can also be its limitations. For example, assessors may be so focused on improvement that they miss imminent threats to the process, such as reliability and validity, or assessors who are fixated on accountability may develop excellent processes but miss opportunities to improve student learning. When an institution values a culture of inquiry and evidence where faculty, students, staff, and community partners take ownership of student learning and fully integrate assessment throughout the fabric of the curriculum, the institution is then able to accomplish the dual purposes of assessment—improvement and accountability.

Setting Assessment Priorities

Depending on the size and scope of the program or institution, undertaking a comprehensive assessment of all outcomes may be a particularly daunting task. Therefore, first and foremost the program or institution should create an assessment committee to facilitate assessment and establish assessment priorities. The committee should discuss, vet, and agree on basic criteria for determining assessment priorities. These criteria may include but are not limited to the college's mission and strategic plan, previous assessment results, innovations, the assessment budget, time for assessment activities, and the impending accreditation deadline. Once the basic criteria have been set, the committee should establish a process for recommending and adopting the final priority focus areas. If possible, the committee should obtain feedback on its priorities from faculty, students, alumni, staff, and administrators.

Factors That Affect Assessment Priorities

The college's mission and strategic plan sets the tone, attitude, and priority for assessment. The shared learning outcomes should be mission driven, meaning that the outcomes should be aligned with the mission and show how they contribute to the achievement of the college's mission. In addition, the college's intentional inclusion of assessment in its strategic plan provides a framework for institutional effectiveness. This becomes a criterion for prioritizing assessment because the college may have set targets and/or benchmarks for student achievement and institutional effectiveness. Therefore, it is incumbent on the various assessment committees to gather evidence to support how well the institution is meeting its effectiveness goals.

In a culture of inquiry and evidence, previous assessment findings become a criterion for setting assessment priorities. The assessment results may indicate that the institution or programs are approaching, are moving away from, have met, or have exceeded the established targets or assessment goals. Thorough analysis and interpretation of assessment findings will direct the course of action or next steps to take. For example, the assessment results may have indicated a decline in a particular skill for students in a particular program. After further analysis of the curriculum maps, the assessment process, the assessment tasks, and the sampling technique, the program would create an intervention to increase student attainment of that skill. The use of the results and assessment of the effectiveness of the intervention may be a priority for the next assessment cycle.

Although the assessment committees have created comprehensive assessment plans, conducting such large-scale assessments may not be practical. In fact, it might be a downright daunting and overwhelming task and the budget may not allow the scope of the plan. Therefore, budget and scope of the assessment might be criteria for prioritizing what needs to be accomplished. Time is another criterion. Assessment is time bound. Realistically, how much time do assessment committees have to accomplish their assessment goals? When is the accrediting report due? Do the college and its various programs have three to five years of assessment data? The answer to these questions may change or establish some assessment priorities. Finally, accountability may be an assessment priority. The principles of accreditation for regional and specialized accrediting bodies require all programs including general education to identify college-level learning outcomes or competencies and assess those outcomes.

Once the newly established shared learning outcomes and assessment priorities have been determined, the institution should communicate this information to various stakeholders. The college should use multiple means of communication to reach the various stakeholders. What structures are already in place to communicate college news or information? There are a number of ways to communicate to the stakeholders and each mode of communication has its own strengths and limitations. For example, when communicating internally the institution may use e-mail blasts, newsletters, or town hall meetings. The institution should also build a dedicated web page for its learning outcomes assessment initiative. Not only is the web page a good way to communicate to external and internal stakeholders about the institution's assessment priorities, but it also allows the institution to be transparent while showcasing its sustainable assessment program including plans, evidence of student learning, and good assessment practices. The National Institute for Learning Outcomes Assessment (NILOA) provides an excellent model for institutions that wish to be transparent: "The NILOA Transparency Framework is intended to help institutions evaluate the extent to which they are making evidence of student accomplishment readily accessible and potentially useful and meaningful to various audiences" (NILOA, 2011). The transparency framework consists of six components of SLO assessment: student learning outcomes, assessment plans, assessment resources, current assessment activities, evidence of student learning, and use of student learning evidence.

Thinking About Activity

The institution has undergone a revision of its general education curriculum and has established six new general education outcomes. Brainstorm and list the criteria that will be used to prioritize the assessment of these outcomes. Then rank the criteria and apply them to develop your assessment priority.

Conclusion

Whether attributed to Hillary Rodham Clinton or an African proverb, assessment takes a village, which includes both academic affairs and student services. As practitioners, we have provided strategies for building shared learning outcomes and determining assessment priorities. Assessment has been characterized as a messy process (Nunley, Bers, & Manning, 2011), and this description is appropriate if an institution has not established a systematic assessment process. Therefore, community and two-year colleges should consider implementing some of these strategies in order to ensure robust outcomes-based assessment practices throughout the institution.

References

Angelo, T. A. (2002). Engaging and supporting faculty in the scholarship of assessment: Guidelines from research and best practice. In T. Banta (Ed.), *Building a scholarship of assessment* (pp. 185–222). San Francisco, CA: Jossey-Bass.

Banta, T. W., Black, K. E., Kahn, S., & Jackson, J. E. (2004, Summer). A perspective on good practice in community college assessment. *New Directions for Community Colleges, 126,* 5–12. doi:10.1002/cc.150

Díaz-Lefebvre, R. (2003, August). In the trenches: Assessment as if understanding mattered. *Learning Abstracts, 6*(8). Retrieved from http://www.league.org/istreamSite/abstracts_index.cfm?url=learning/lelabs0308.htm

Hutchings, P. (2010, April). *Opening doors to faculty involvement in assessment* (NILOA Occasional Paper No. 4). Urbana, IL: University of Illinois and Indiana University, National Institute for Learning Outcomes Assessment. Retrieved from http://learningoutcomeassessment.org/documents/PatHutchings.pdf

Hutchings, P. (2011, Spring). *What new faculty need to know about assessment* (Assessment Brief: Faculty). Urbana, IL: University of Illinois and Indiana University, National Institute for Learning Outcomes Assessment. Retrieved from http://www.learningoutcomesassessment.org/documents/ABfaculty.pdf

Kezar, A. (2001, Winter). Documenting the landscape: Results of a national study on academic and student affairs collaborations. *New Directions for Higher Education, 116,* 39–51. doi:10.1002/he.32

Kotter, J. P. (1996). *Leading change.* Boston, MA: Harvard Business School Press.

Maki, P. L. (2004). *Assessing for learning: Building a sustainable commitment across the institution.* Sterling, VA: Stylus.

National Governors Association Center for Best Practices, Council of Chief State School Officers. (2010). *Implementing the common core state standards.* Washington, DC: Author. Retrieved from http://www.corestandards.org/

National Institute for Learning Outcomes Assessment. (2011). *Transparency framework.* Urbana, IL: University of Illinois and Indiana University, National Institute for Learning Outcomes Assessment. Retrieved from: http://www.learningoutcomeassessment.org/TransparencyFramework.htm

Nunley, C., Bers, T., & Manning, T. (2011, July). *Learning outcomes assessment in community colleges* (NILOA Occasional Paper No. 10). Urbana, IL: University of Illinois and Indiana University, National Institute for Learning Outcomes Assessment. Retrieved from http://www.learningoutcomeassessment.org/documents/CommunityCollege.pdf

Palomba, C. A., & Banta, T. W. (1999). *Assessment essentials: Planning, implementing, and improving assessment in higher education.* San Francisco, CA: Jossey-Bass.

Schuh, J. H., & Upcraft, M. L. (2001). *Assessment practice in student affairs: An applications manual.* San Francisco, CA: Jossey-Bass.

Suskie, L. (2009). *Assessing student learning: A common sense guide* (2nd ed.). San Francisco, CA: Jossey-Bass.

University of Hawai'i at Mānoa. (2013). *Assessment how-to: Curriculum mapping/ curriculum matrix.* Retrieved from http://manoa.hawaii.edu/assessment/howto/ mapping.htm

Walvoord, B. E. (2010). *Assessment clear and simple: A practical guide for institutions, departments, and general education* (2nd ed.). San Francisco, CA: Jossey-Bass.

Webb, N. L. (1997, April). *Criteria for alignment of expectations and assessments in mathematics and science education* (Council of Chief State School Officers and National Institute for Science Education Research Monograph No. 6). Madison, WI: University of Wisconsin, Wisconsin Center for Education Research. Retrieved from http://facstaff.wceruw.org/normw/WEBBMonograph6criteria.pdf

Suggested Reading

Kotter, J. P. (1996). *Leading change.* Boston, MA: Harvard Business School Press.

Schuh, J. H., & Associates. (2008). *Assessment methods for student affairs.* San Francisco, CA: Jossey-Bass.

Suskie, L. (2009). *Assessing student learning: A common sense guide* (2nd ed.). San Francisco, CA: Jossey-Bass.

Tagg, J. (2003). *The learning paradigm college.* Bolton, MA: Anker.

Walvoord, B. E. (2010). *Assessment clear and simple: A practical guide for institutions, departments, and general education* (2nd ed.). San Francisco, CA: Jossey-Bass.

4

BUILDING A PROFESSIONAL DEVELOPMENT PLAN

Virginia Taylor

The growing interest in outcomes-based assessment coupled with the culture of evidence expected from accreditation agencies has significantly increased the pressures on community and two-year college professionals to document, measure, and assess the effectiveness of an array of academic and student services. These pressures have forced campus administrators to turn to division leaders and department managers to develop and implement comprehensive reviews of all services provided to students. Although many of these individuals may be underprepared to develop a comprehensive assessment plan, the principles of plan, act, assess, react, and improve can be learned through the creation and completion of a multifaceted professional development plan. I have written this chapter with the novice practitioner or faculty member in mind; however, it may also be of interest to those of us currently engaged in assessment and endeavoring to get it "just" right.

Building Foundational Skills Through Self-Assessment

Depending on the extent of your assessment experience, the self-assessment process should have at least three steps. The first step is to assess what you and/or your faculty and student services personnel already know. What undergraduate or graduate statistics, measurement and appraisal, or assessment courses or workshops have already been completed? Can any of the material learned or resources used in these courses be utilized in current assessment processes? The second step is to consider your work experiences. Has the clinical experience of providing student services contributed to the understanding of what works (or does not work) when trying to motivate community college students? What does or does not work to demonstrate learning in the classroom effectively? The third step is to determine whether any previously completed professional development activities (conferences, seminars, webinars, etc.) can be utilized in the creation of a professional development plan.

Seeking Out New Learning Opportunities

Once the self-assessment task is completed, the next step is to determine whether further education or training in the field of assessment is necessary. A good first step is to join a state, regional, or national organization that focuses on student assessment. Some of the more valuable organizations for both faculty and student services practitioners are College Student Educators International, the Educational Policy Institute, the National Council on Student Development, the Association for the Study of Higher Education, the American Educational Research Association, the Association for Institutional Research, and Student Affairs Administrators in Higher Education (NASPA). Although not directly related to student services programming or the academic classroom, another very interesting organization to consider is the Society for College and University Planning (SCUP). As with many professional organizations, if your campus is a member of SCUP, the assessment-related materials are very inexpensive or offered at no cost. These professional organizations also routinely offer seminars and conferences that will help to sharpen your planning and assessment skills. These seminars and conferences are an excellent means of garnering and sharing resources and picking up current or best practice ideas that can be implemented on your campus.

Another angle is to determine who the experts are in the assessment field and read through their contributions to the literature. It adds credibility to your assessment knowledge to have talking points that provide an illustration of your approach. By saying something such as, "Our division of student affairs meshes the approaches of Alexander Astin, John Schuh, and Marilee Bresciani. I have some of their books in my office if you would ever like to borrow them," you are opening up a two-way dialogue regarding assessment, making it more human. In addition, taking the time to build a library of resource materials will result in a significant payoff when engaging in the process of assessment. If your campus is fortunate to have a standalone office of institutional research or assessment, see what resources are available to utilize during the assessment process.

If funds are tight, journal articles and book chapters can be downloaded from the web for free or books can be borrowed through the campus interlibrary loan service. In addition to some of the more recent publications, there are at least six national organizations that have assessment resources readily available on the web:

1. Association for Institutional Research (www.airweb.org)
2. College Student Educators International (ACPA) Commission for Assessment and Evaluation (www2.myacpa.org/acpa-commission-for-assessment -and-evaluation-home)
3. Community College Survey of Student Engagement (www.ccsse.org)
4. Council for the Advancement of Standards in Higher Education (www .cas.edu)
5. National Community College Benchmark Project (www.nccbp.org)
6. NASPA (www.naspa.org)

Another way to get started on your educational journey is to read current articles, documents, reports, or publications on assessment. Figure 4.1 provides an example of direct links to materials that can be found by simply using Google Scholar.

Hiring guest speakers or consultants is also an excellent way to improve the assessment knowledge base of an individual, the department, or the division. Consider participating in web-based professional development activities such as podcasts or webinars. Assessment webinars can be purchased from either www. studentaffairs.com/webinars/ orwww.paper-clip.com/ME2/Default.asp. Likewise, although not widely available, there may be graduate opportunities to register for a single class on assessment or apply for entrance into a graduate program that is focused on education assessment.

Gaining Expertise Through Nontraditional Means

Working directly with someone who has the expertise you are striving for can help you to improve skills in the area of assessment. One of the benefits of working on a college campus is the wealth of knowledge people have and their willingness to share what they know. When evaluating the effectiveness of the community and two-year college experience, it is important to consider academic and student services administrators and faculty who would be willing to collaborate and share their insights on assessment. Another way to gain insights is to volunteer to be a member of the institutional accreditation team. These teams tend to be made up of talented

Figure 4.1 Examples of direct link texts on assessment found online.

Debra D. Bragg and Brian Durham - Perspectives on Access and Equity in the Era of (Community) College Completion http://crw.sagepub.com/content/ 40/2/106.full.pdf+html

Marilee J. Bresciani - Understanding Barriers to Student Affairs Professionals' Engagement in Outcomes-Based Assessment of Student Learning and Development www.sahe.colostate.edu/Data/Sites/1/documents/journal/2010_Journal _of_Student_Affairs.pdf#page=83

George D. Kuh and Peter T. Ewell - The State of Learning Outcomes Assessment in the United States www.units.muohio.edu/celt/events/docs/CFLING/ state%20of%20learning%20outcomes%20assessment%20in%20the%20us.pdf

Peter T. Ewell - The Lumina Degree Qualifications Profile (DQP): Implications for Assessment www.learningoutcomesassessment.org/documents/DQPop1.pdf

Charlene Nunley, Trudy Bers, and Terri Manning - Learning Outcomes Assessment in Community Colleges www.learningoutcomesassessment.org/docu ments/CommunityCollege.pdf

John H. Schuh and Ann M. Gansemer-Topf - The Role of Student Affairs in Student Learning Assessment www.sc.edu/fye/research/assessment_resources/ pdf/StudentAffairsRole.pdf

Vincent Tinto - Taking Student Retention Seriously: Rethinking the First Year of University www.yorku.ca/retentn/rdata/Takingretentionseriously.pdf

individuals who are very knowledgeable and experienced in the areas of assessment and accountability. Mentoring is another possible avenue for gaining expertise. If your campus has a formal mentoring system, contact the program administrator to see what options are available to you. If no formal program exists, seek out a mentor on your own. If no appropriate mentor can be found on your campus, consider soliciting a mentorship at another institution in your area or one that is similar in size, structure, and culture to your own.

What Works: Thinking Through the Process of Assessment

In 1998, John Schuh posted an article on NASPA's website entitled "Getting Started—An Assessment Challenge." While this motivational article had some very practical guidance about getting started in assessment, it also provided a "road map" to assessment success for the student services professional:

- Pick a manageable project.
- Pick a topic in which your supervisor has an interest.
- Pick a project where you have the technical expertise.
- Pick a project where staff can help.
- Pick a project where you will look good. (Schuh, 1998)

Though this road map was geared for the student services professional, these words of wisdom can be applied in both cocurricular and academic settings. Employing this advice will assist community and two-year college professionals in managing the competing goals and priorities of twenty-first-century educational institutions. Assessment results can be used to ensure that what we do does matter in the life of a student, that we are serving as many students as effectively as possible, and that we are balancing the needs of students within the budgetary and human resource constraints that we face. Assessment results will also aid in our endeavor to uncover unmet student needs and may help administrators and faculty make the case for additional resources in their respective areas.

Getting Started: The Creation of an Assessment Work Group

Whether you decide to start a work group on your own or a campus administrator has assigned this task as an "other duties" task, not only will the use of a highly structured approach reduce stress, but it can also significantly improve the overall success of the endeavor. Before the first meeting is called, consider implementing all of the following "getting started" suggestions:

1. Determine what is to be assessed. Is the assessment a departmental, divisional, or institutional undertaking? Is there an interest in assessing a single academic or student service or program? If so, which one is going to be assessed? If more than three programs or services are to be assessed, a timeline or cycle will need to be established.
2. Determine the goals of the assessment work group. In addition to evaluating the effectiveness of a program or service, can the work be tied to a departmental, divisional, or institutional strategic goal; the campus strategic plan; or an accreditation review? If so, additional resources may be available for the asking.

3. Determine the group membership. Who should be invited to partici-pate? Should folks outside the area be included? What is the role or responsibility of each of the members? Because you will need access to data and reports, consider recruiting individuals from the information technology and institutional research areas. When the time comes to set the first meeting date, think about who should extend invitation to the participants. An invitation from a vice president or a dean will set a tone of importance and significance.

4. Determine the tools and resources that will be necessary to ensure the success of the assessment process. Access to student-level and summary data and reports is crucial to the success of any assessment endeavor. Be sure that the group has access to what is needed. Also, if applicable, at least one member of the group should have access to the campus-supported assessment tool, such as TracDat. If available, provide the results of any previously completed student services evaluations, including, but not limited to, student survey results. One of the ways to ensure quick progress to task completion is to have a guidebook available with all the necessary tools (glossaries, worksheets, templates, reporting formats, etc.). Because the goal is to create an assessment plan, have examples available from other colleges that closely approxi-mate what the final product should look like. If you have difficulty finding suitable examples, check the websites of colleges in your region/ system or look at community colleges in states that have assessment reports readily available for review such as Oregon, Arizona, Florida, or Virginia.

5. Consider the assessment knowledge level of the group members. If a few members need training, try imbedding the basic principles into the regular meeting schedule. Another idea is to consider dedicating 15 minutes per meeting for topical presentations from campus (or local) assessment experts. If the entire group needs training and the financial resources are available, try combining training and creation of the first draft of the assessment plan by organizing a full-day retreat.

Conclusion

There is no doubt that implementing an outcomes-based assessment for an academic or student services program or department can be a daunting task. Because the key to success in creating and implementing an assessment plan relies heavily on the skill set of the program or department manager, the goal of this chapter was to present a collection of professional development activities designed to improve one's assessment-related skills and knowledge base. Interest in the field of assessment, especially as it relates to the services and programs at the community and two-year college, is becoming more pronounced with each passing year. This interest will potentially fuel an exponential growth in the literature, which will be immensely helpful to community college educators now and in the future. As current practitioners, it is incumbent on each of us not only to stay current and practice what is learned, but also to share the knowledge gained through mentoring the next generation of student affairs professionals.

Reference

Schuh, J.H. (1998). Making a difference: The centerpiece of current assessment issues. *Net Results: The NASPA Leadership and Strategy Magazine, 2.* Published electronically without page numbers.

5

SELECTING A METHOD

Victoria Livingston, David Phillips, and Kimberly A. Kline

When selecting an assessment method, the first step in the process is identifying the purpose of the assessment. Frequently, assessment is conducted because staff and faculty believe it is something they "have to do" or "must do," and not because they can identify a real need. When assessments are motivated by these intentions, data are collected just for the sake of doing so. Once collected, this information is frequently useless at both the programmatic/service level and the larger division/institutional level (Banta, Jones, & Black, 2009). Because there was no intention behind *why* the data were being collected, it becomes very difficult to give the data purpose after the fact. The staff or faculty who collected the data will have trouble determining the usefulness of the information because they were never able to articulate how it would benefit their program in the first place. Administrators will be unable to use it for decision making because it is highly unlikely to connect to strategic priorities. In the end, there must be intention behind any assessment that is implemented (Bresciani, Moore Gardner, & Hickmott, 2009; Palomba & Banta, 1999). Identifying the purpose of the assessment at the beginning of the process helps ensure that the information being collected is valuable and vital to bettering the program and services of the college.

Defining the purpose of the assessment does not have to be a particularly painstaking process. Schuh, Upcraft, and Associates (2001) broke the process into two steps: (a) defining the problem the assessment is seeking to answer, and (b), based on the problem, identifying the purpose of the assessment. For them, the purpose of the assessment is the information that is needed to solve the problem. Identifying the purpose of the process can even be a much simpler process of looking to guiding documents, such as the mission or strategic planning documents, and using them to identify the core tasks and purposes of the department. Generally, these are the efforts that will be assessed regularly. Program or learning outcomes can also be used to help articulate the purpose of an assessment.

Guiding and Planning Documents

The purpose of an assessment is often determined by guiding and/or planning documents. These documents outline the purpose behind the work being done and the vision for where those efforts should be in the future. In short, guiding and planning documents communicate "what the institution values and what it aspires to be" (Middaugh, 2010, p. 23). These documents serve the same purpose whether they are written for an institution, a division, a department, or an office. Because guiding and planning documents look to the future, they provide critical guidance for the type of information an assessment should gather.

At a departmental level, mission and vision statements, annual goals, and strategic plans can all be excellent sources of direction. For example, a director is looking to better the services that her department offers to the nontraditional student population. She also knows that her department has a strategic priority aimed at increasing outreach to minority students. Based on this strategic priority, she may decide that the purpose of this assessment is to learn about the needs of nontraditional minority students and how her department could provide better outreach. This is an example of using guiding/foundational documents to inform assessment that will be meaningful to the department and its vision for where it wants to be in the future.

In institutional documents, the language is broader and meant to apply to both academic and administrative areas. For someone working at the department level, it is necessary to take these broad concepts and focus them into something that is relevant to the work of one area. To do this, one must first articulate what the institutional priority looks like for the specific program, service, or course that is being assessed. Assessments without these specific connections can easily become too big and generate information that is too broad and generic to be useful. This focusing process is critical because it is part of what helps make the results actionable. In the best-case scenario, the departmental guiding documents are written with the institutional documents in mind so that those connections will already be made; however, occasionally, new institutional initiatives are developed, and it becomes necessary to make these connections retroactively so that they are measurable at the programmatic level.

Learning and Program/Operational Outcomes

Guiding and planning documents will often contain specific learning outcomes and program/operational outcomes. These can also be extremely beneficial when identifying the purpose of an assessment because they provide specific criteria for success. As outlined in chapter 3, good outcomes are written in such a way that they can be easily measured. Therefore, the purpose of an assessment could be to assess whether the stated outcomes are being met. A faculty member could use certain classroom assessments to measure whether students are achieving a programwide critical thinking outcome. Similarly, a staff member could utilize a rubric to evaluate student leader reflection essays in order to determine whether key leadership outcomes were met. Because outcomes are written with the intention of connecting back to guiding/planning documents (Bresciani et al., 2009), they can be used to determine course/program effectiveness and for decision making.

Criteria to Consider When Selecting a Method

Before selecting an assessment method, there are several key considerations to take into account. Every method has its own advantages and disadvantages and, depending on the type of data you wish to collect, one method may be more appropriate than others in certain situations. The answers to the questions addressed in the following sections will assist you in selecting the most appropriate method given the circumstances. It should be noted that these guiding questions and their proposed answers cannot be considered hard-and-fast rules but are useful for most situations.

How Will the Results Be Used?

Once the purpose of the assessment has been decided, the next question to ask is: How will the results be used to inform current endeavors and/or effect improvement? The answer depends on who are the key stakeholders of the assessment. While the results of the assessment may be shared with many different stakeholders, the key audience will fall into one of three categories: decision makers, action takers, and interested parties. The key audience will determine the extent to which your method should be suited to collecting quantitative or qualitative data.

Decision makers will often be those in key leadership positions and responsible for overseeing multiple academic or administrative units. Decision makers are generally interested in seeing quantitative data. Quantitative data are numeric data, which can be analyzed using statistical analysis and are often reported in the aggregate (Bresciani et al., 2009). Such data are best at answering questions with finite answer choices, such as who, what, where, and when. Decision makers often need these quick facts that can be easily distilled down into a few essential data points to inform administrative and financial decisions.

Utilizing quantitative data is quicker and more efficient for decision makers because it is easier to communicate to others and can be used to demonstrate overall effectiveness. Quantitative data are also preferable for those in key leadership positions because it is easier to make comparisons and generalize numbers across functional areas. Within this context, decision makers may also include task forces and/or campus committees charged with gathering a great breadth of information on a particular topic of interest in order to make institution-wide recommendations.

On the other hand, *action takers* are the ones who often work at the programmatic or service level. Action takers will be more interested in context-specific information. Qualitative data provide more contextual-based, narrative information on the specific topic being studied (Bresciani et al., 2009). They will provide greater insight into the behaviors, beliefs, and perceptions of one's respondents. Action takers will want to know not only the who, what, where, and when of the assessment, but also the why and how. This descriptive, qualitative information will be of more importance to those at the programmatic or service level because it offers a deeper understanding of how respondents are reacting to the topic being assessed. It will give a more detailed picture of how effective the services/programs are and provide specific ways in which they can be improved.

It is also important to acknowledge the existence of other stakeholders. Community and two-year colleges in particular develop close ties to regional businesses and governments that may be interested in certain types of assessment results. Students also have a vested interest in knowing that their college is striving to perform at its very best. Therefore, it is important to consider what information these *interested parties* need to know and what would be the most powerful way to share it with them. Often these individuals or groups will be most interested in seeing quantitative information that is presented in a concise format. These stakeholders will not be invested in reading or making sense of long, dense reports but will instead want information that is more easily digested. This group will often prefer quantitative data because it will enable them to learn about the big picture without getting bogged down in the details.

Although taking into account one's audience provides some general guidance concerning the types of data to collect, there will always be exceptions to the generalizations just discussed; therefore, it is important to use your best judgment when determining what kind of information to gather. Furthermore, there may be many situations in which there are various intended audiences for the assessment results. In such situations, it is best to consider using a mixed-methods assessment, or conducting more than one assessment on the same topic in order to collect multidimensional data that will appeal to the informational needs of multiple groups of stakeholders.

Who Are the Potential Respondents?

The next question to consider is: Given the purpose of the assessment, who are the potential respondents? Or, who is best suited to answer questions about, or provide information on, the subject of the assessment? There are two key factors to consider when determining the level of influence the potential respondents will have on method selection. The respondents' level of contact with the individual or group conducting the assessment and their level of investment in the subject of the assessment will greatly influence the potential success of various methods. These two factors can help determine the level of commitment respondents will have when completing an assessment. Figure 5.1 illustrates the four various groups into which the respondents could fall. Each of the groups will be more or less committed to completing certain types of assessment.

Typically, assessments that focus on a particular service or program are the ones that have respondents who fall into the *high-contact* category. These respondents would be considered high contact because they have a great deal of connection with the person or group who is administering the assessment. For example, student employees and students who hold leadership roles are likely to be a high-contact group. In a community or two-year college where students tend to be more nontraditional and less involved (Cohen & Brawer, 2008), it may be more difficult to find students who fall into this category; however, there will always be pockets of high-contact students and subpopulations. Academic classroom assessment may also be considered high contact because academic classes meet on a regular basis and have an obligatory term-long relationship.

Low-contact respondents are individuals with whom there is little or no relationship between the student and the person or group conducting the assessment. It can be difficult to get this group of respondents to complete an assessment; therefore, it is particularly important to consider the length and complexity of any assessment methods that are chosen for this group.

Figure 5.1 Types of respondents.

		Investment	
		High	Low
Contact	High	High contact High investment	High contact Low investment
	Low	Low contact High investment	Low contact Low investment

Assessments done with low-contact respondents tend to be larger division/ collegewide assessments that assess multiple functional areas at one time. They can often also be nonuser assessments.

Although the respondent group's tendency to be either high or low contact can be relatively easy to judge, it can be more difficult to determine whether the group will have high or low investment. Integral to this idea of high versus low investment is a statement from Palomba and Banta (1999): "It is important to choose instruments that will be valuable for students and that will elicit their cooperation" (p. 92). If students do not understand the value of an assessment, they will commit less time and energy to completing it. A respondent will have *high investment* if it is a topic in which they have a greater personal stake. This can be because they are already highly involved or interested in the subject of the assessment or because the results of the assessment have the possibility of greatly impacting their quality of student life. On the opposite end of the spectrum, a respondent will have *low investment* if it is a topic about which they will have very little at stake. Although it can be difficult to determine, the respondents' perceived level of investment could help inform method selection. This concept of high and low investment would also hold true for any nonstudent respondent group including parents, staff, faculty, or community members.

It would be easy to make the assumption that all high-contact respondents will also be high investment and vice versa; however, this would be incorrect. For example, if an assessment was done on the availability of campus child care options and was sent to all students who are parents of young children, this would be an example of a low-contact, high-investment respondent group. As parents, these students are likely to fall into the nontraditional student population and be less involved on campus. They are also likely to be spread out across campus without many other common identifiers other than the fact that they are students and they are parents. Therefore, this respondent group is likely to be low contact. Nevertheless, they would have a high investment in the availability of campus child care. Knowing that they are likely to have a high investment is important because it makes them more likely to participate in a longer, involved assessment.

There are also situations in which the assessment may call for assessing two vastly different populations with different levels of investment and contact. For example, an assessment of campus safety may call for assessing students as well as faculty and staff. There will be situations, like a campus safety assessment, that will allow use of the same assessment on all respondents regardless of the group into which they fall. There will be other situations when it will make more sense to utilize different assessment methods based on the population in which respondents belong. If an assessment is done to assess satisfaction with a new class registration process, it makes the most sense to send a survey to students who would fall into the low-contact, high-investment group, but conduct focus groups with faculty who will fall into a high-contact, high-investment group. Faculty will have greater knowledge of the process and how it impacts their day-to-day work, which, therefore, means that it is beneficial to assess them using a more involved method.

What Resources Are Available?

The day-to-day reality of working on a campus, especially a community or two-year college, is that inevitably there will never be enough resources to accomplish everything that is desired or needed, including assessment. Thus, the third question that must be asked when selecting an assessment method is: What resources are *actually* available to conduct this assessment? There are three categories of resources—money, time, and knowledge/expertise—which we discuss next.

Money is one of the first resource concerns that come to mind when planning to conduct an assessment. Some types of assessment may require greater financial investment than others. Participating in nationally benchmarked studies, subscribing to data management or survey administration tools, purchasing prizes/incentives, or even simply paying for copying fees can all have an impact on a department's bottom line. Any assessment will likely have some financial aspect, but it is not necessary to invest a great deal of money in order to do worthwhile assessment. Although money should not greatly influence the type of method that is selected, it might influence the scope of the project. Instead of paying to conduct a nationally standardized survey, one might instead create a locally developed survey.

The second resource is *time*. This is often the time put in by staff and faculty when planning, administering, and analyzing an assessment; however, it could also refer to time in the academic year. Anyone who has worked on a campus knows that there are never enough hours in the day, or staff in the office, to accomplish everything that needs to get done. Therefore, time can be a critical barrier to conducting worthwhile assessment (Palomba & Banta, 1999). Surveys are often a culprit of time-crunched, poorly planned assessment because they are familiar and relatively easy to produce. Nevertheless, even a survey requires some time to create. This is especially true when one is trying to conduct intentional high-quality assessment. Therefore, it is critical to set aside the time to plan and conduct assessment, including taking into account the time of the academic year. There are certain times, such as the beginning/end of the semester and breaks, when it is inadvisable to conduct an assessment because everyone's attention will be focused on other things.

In addition, some methods may require more work on the development end whereas others may require a greater commitment in terms of conducting the analysis. This allowance for time must be built into one's schedule for the academic year. It is helpful to make sure that key leaders are informed of and invested in the assessment being conducted in order to ensure that ample time can be set aside to do it correctly.

The final resource is staff *knowledge/expertise*. Depending on the method being considered, it might be necessary to seek out additional education or professional development in order to learn how to develop, conduct, or analyze an assessment properly. For example, many student affairs staff are less familiar with utilizing rubrics in assessment. If a rubric is the method that best fits the assessment's needs, it will be necessary to seek out opportunities for professional development and/or collaboration with faculty in order to administer it correctly. Assessment-focused professional development is a powerful way to increase the effectiveness and caliber of assessment (Banta et al., 2009). It not only educates staff and faculty as to the variety of assessment options available to them, but also increases their confidence in their ability to do assessment. Chapter 4 discusses how to develop an assessment professional development plan in greater depth; however, when on-campus professional development opportunities are not available, additional sources of knowledge/expertise may include other professionals who have the requisite experience, educational opportunities at conferences, and available literature.

All of these logistical considerations culminate in the fact that, regardless of the assessment being done or the method being chosen, you must always assess wisely. It is recommended to occasionally take inventory of the multitude of assessments being done within your division or institution (Palomba & Banta, 1999). This can help limit the amount of repetitive work and assessment that is done across the institution. Even within one's own functional area, resources are too scarce to do the same assessment on the same program/service every single year. In her book *Sudden Death*, Rita Mae Brown (1984) said, "Insanity is doing the same thing, over and over again, but expecting different results" (p. 68). Unless the course, program, or service delivery has changed dramatically from one year to the next, assessment results are unlikely to change dramatically within the span of one year. Therefore, even though it is always beneficial to be able to show longitudinal trends, data can be collected every few years rather than annually.

It is also possible to assess wisely by seeking out additional resources on campus. Collaborating with other departments that have similar assessment needs can be a great place to start. In addition, master's- and doctoral-level student interns can be a source of knowledge and time for a department that does not have enough human resources to plan for or analyze its own assessment.

What Type of Information Will the Assessment Be Gathering?

There are various types of information that can be gathered through an assessment. Some of the more common types are satisfaction, needs, usage, effectiveness, learning outcomes, culture/climate, and benchmarking. Nearly all of these can be assessed using multiple types of methods. Some, such as satisfaction, are often assessed using surveys; however, satisfaction can also be assessed using a focus group, a reflective journal, or observation. Therefore, the final question when selecting a method is: What type of information will the assessment be gathering? If the answer is longitudinal or learning assessment, there are some final considerations to take into account.

Longitudinal Data

If information has previously been collected on a subject and longitudinal data are needed, the original method of data collection must be used. To be able to compare trends over time, it is necessary to collect the same type of information in the same format so that those comparisons can be made in a reliable way. For example, if the original study utilized a survey, one would not want to drastically change the questions on the survey or even use a different method altogether because it would be extremely difficult, if not impossible, to directly compare one year's results to the next.

However, if one is looking to collect information on the same subject but use it to further inform or elucidate the original study, then it is okay, and even advisable, to select a method that is different. This is sometimes done when people have additional questions or want to dig deeper after analyzing the results of the original assessment. For example, students who participate in a focus group about ideas for remodeling the campus library may provide a lot of feedback on particular aspects of the potential redesign; however, those who conducted the assessment may have more questions that they need answered and thus might do more focus groups, or a survey, in order to gather that information and further expand on the original information that they collected.

Learning Assessment

Assessing learning is a high priority on most campuses regardless of whether one is talking about curricular or cocurricular learning. Learning can be assessed using a variety of methods; however, these methods can greatly influence the kind of learning assessment that is being done. There are many great sources that discuss learning assessment in more depth, but the most basic consideration is whether one wants to engage in direct or indirect assessment (Palomba & Banta, 1999).

Direct learning assessment requires respondents to directly display their knowledge, behaviors, or skills. Indirect assessment asks students to reflect on their knowledge, behaviors, or skills. Neither of these assessments is better than the other; they merely represent two different ways of going about the same thing. Direct assessment is the type of learning assessment most often seen in classrooms; however, it can be difficult to administer in a cocurricular setting. It is often highly valued because it enables the assessor to make judgments about whether respondents have *actually* learned what they were supposed to. The assessor can examine the display of knowledge, behavior, or skills and evaluate whether evidence of learning is present. In indirect learning assessment, one is relying on respondents' perception of how much they have learned. This is, obviously, open to some error because respondents may believe that they know more or less than they actually do. Certain methods lend themselves more readily to direct or indirect learning assessment. It is important to decide what type of learning assessment needs to be conducted so that an appropriate method can be selected.

Methods

The Selecting a Method Decision-Making Grid (see Table 5.1) lists the four key questions one must answer when selecting a method and demonstrates how they relate to four common methods that can be utilized in curricular or cocurricular assessment. Although this is not an exhaustive list of potential assessment methods, these four methods are arguably the most common. The grid should be considered a general guideline for selecting an appropriate method depending on the context of a specific assessment. Nevertheless, be critical when utilizing the grid because there could always be exceptions based on extenuating circumstances.

Augmenting the information available in Table 5.1, the following sections discuss surveys, focus groups/interviews, and other additional considerations in greater detail.

Surveys

Perhaps one of the most common forms of assessment, surveys are ubiquitous on college campuses. They provide quick feedback on programs and services without necessarily requiring a great deal of resource investment. Surveys can be an optimal choice when attempting to assess low-contact, low-investment respondents because if they are written correctly surveys require very little time and effort on the part of respondents. To this end, it is important to keep surveys very focused on the topic that is being assessed and

TABLE 5.1
Selecting a Method Decision-Making Grid

	How will the results be used?	Who are the potential respondents? (see Figure 5.1)	What resources are available?	What type of information will the assessment be gathering?
Surveys	Primarily collects quantitative data Data often used by decision makers, action takers, and interested parties	Best suited for low-contact and low-investment groups, but would work for any of the groups outlined in Figure 5.1	Can be done with minimal time, money, and expertise May require money if purchasing an externally developed instrument or service	Well suited for longitudinal tracking Can be used to collect indirect learning assessment but are not well suited for direct learning assessment
Focus Groups and Interviews	Primarily collects qualitative data Data often used by action takers	Best suited for high-investment groups because of the greater time commitment required of participants	Requires more time and expertise to facilitate the focus groups and/ or interviews and to conduct the qualitative data analysis once the data are collected	Not advised for longitudinal tracking Interviews particularly useful for direct assessment of learning
Rubrics (Observation and Artifact Analysis)	Collects quantitative and qualitative data equally well Data most often used by action takers, but aggregate quantitative data may be shared with decision makers	An *observation rubric* successfully utilized with any of the groups in Figure 5.1 An *artifact analysis* rubric best used with high-investment groups unless one is evaluating preexisting artifacts (e.g., student newspaper)	Requires time and expertise to create a well-written rubric and to collect data through observation and/or analysis; less time needed for data analysis	Quantitative data useful for longitudinal tracking Very well suited for direct assessment of learning
External Benchmarking	Primarily collects quantitative data Data often used by decision makers and action takers	Unique because it is collecting data from other institutions, not students; however, same rules apply Best used with institutions where there is high contact and/or high investment in the topic because they will be more likely to respond	Minimal money or expertise needed if the data are being collected internally but requires time to reach out to potential respondents May require significantly more money to purchase an externally or commercially developed benchmarking project	Well suited for longitudinal tracking Learning assessment not applicable

limit superfluous questions. The longer and more complicated the survey, the more attrition there will be among respondents.

Surveys are particularly well suited to gathering quantitative information because they can collect a large amount of information within a short space of time. As stated previously, quantitative assessment is good at measuring straightforward, basic information that answers questions such as who, what, where, and when. The use of multiple-choice questions gives respondents the ability to answer quickly and efficiently. In addition, multiple-choice answer options make it easier to analyze the results because one does not have to go through and analyze a long list of open-ended responses. This makes surveys preferable for individuals who do not have as much time to spend analyzing their assessment results.

Although you can gather some qualitative information through surveys, it is important to limit the number of questions with open-ended answers. They will require more effort on the part of the respondent, and the qualitative information that is gathered will not be as meaningful or in depth as data gathered through other methods better suited to qualitative measures. Because they are well suited to collecting quantitative information, surveys also make it easy to collect longitudinal data. The quantitative nature of surveys also means that they can collect indirect measurement of learning but are not well suited to direct assessment of learning. Respondents will be much more likely to mark an answer to a Likert-type question about how much they think they learned than they would be to answer an open-ended question asking them to display that knowledge directly.

Depending on the type of survey being administered, a varying amount of resources will need to be dedicated to it. Many nationally standardized surveys are available to institutions, but there is typically a fee for administering them. Regardless, nationally standardized surveys can be a good option for institutions that want to use an instrument that has had its reliability and validity tested and to have access to the comparable data (Palomba & Banta, 1999). Locally developed surveys, on the other hand, will require staff and faculty time and expertise to develop; however, they will be crafted to reflect the unique considerations of that campus (Palomba & Banta, 1999). Money may also play a part in deciding how to administer a survey. A small fee may be associated with copying costs if it is to be administered via paper and pencil, or a subscription to an online survey system could incur a fee if the data are collected online.

Focus Groups/Interviews

Focus groups and interviews are both particularly well suited at providing in-depth qualitative information. For the purposes of this chapter, they have been lumped together because the considerations one must take into account before administering them are very similar. At its most basic, the format of a focus group or interview consists of a facilitator who asks a participant, or small group of participants, questions on a particular topic. This format allows the assessor to gain detailed feedback. Focus groups and interviews are particularly useful at providing context and narrative to help illustrate whatever topic is being discussed. A critical element of a focus group or interview is the development of a facilitator/interviewer protocol. This protocol helps ensure that the qualitative data are collected in as consistent a way as possible and that the results can be documented and analyzed. The protocol is what separates casual interactions in which a staff or faculty member might ask students questions from a legitimate assessment method.

Potential respondents for a focus group or interview are individuals who have high investment in the assessment topic. As a rule, focus groups and interviews require more from participants because they have to take time out of their daily life to participate. In addition, focus groups and interviews require participants to spend time providing thoughtful answers to the questions that they are asked. Low-investment individuals will be highly unlikely to put forth this kind of effort; therefore, it is important to make sure that participants understand the importance of participating in a focus group or interview. High-contact individuals will be the easiest to recruit for these methods; however, if you can get their attention, low-contact individuals may also be convinced to participate. With focus groups and interviews, more so than surveys, it is important to ensure that you get a representative mix of participants. Because surveys involve a much larger number of participants, it is easier to ensure that all groups are represented. By contrast, in a focus group or interview, these numbers are considerably smaller, which means that you may have to reach out to certain groups.

Time and knowledge/expertise are the two resources that you will want to be aware of when planning a focus group or interview. It takes time not only to develop the protocols and conduct multiple focus groups/interviews, but also to put all of that qualitative information into a useable format and then analyze it. It will be important both to allow ample time for this process and to include someone in the planning team who knows how to analyze qualitative data. This is a good opportunity to seek out peers in other departments, faculty, or even graduate students who have this sort of knowledge and are looking for the experience.

Finally, focus groups and interviews provide the opportunity for direct measures of learning. Because respondents are sitting there with the facilitator, it is possible to ask them learning-based questions and then later analyze the results to determine whether there is evidence of them directly displaying that knowledge. In addition, because the facilitator is talking with respondents in real time, he or she can immediately follow up with them if something is unclear or vague.

Collecting Multidimensional Data

While this chapter has focused on how to select a method for a particular project, it is equally important to consider the diversity of methods employed by one's office, department, or division as a whole. As should be clear at this point, certain methods are better at collecting certain types of information than others. If a department collects assessment data only through surveys, the information will be heavily quantitative and lack much of the context and narrative that qualitative information could provide to help the department better understand its programs and services. On the other hand, if a department collects only qualitative information, it will have very few hard numbers that may be useful to report up to supervisors and administrators and that they themselves might need in order to inform their own decision making. For this reason, it is important to collect multidimensional, or well-rounded, data. Simply varying the assessment methods used will yield a greater depth and breadth of information overall.

Ethics

Whenever conducting assessment, it is absolutely essential to conduct that assessment in an ethical manner. As with any other kind of work, assessment is susceptible to lack of knowledge and/or the influence of organizational politics (see the next section for a more thorough analysis of organizational politics) and the unethical decisions that can sometimes be produced as a result. To maintain good assessment ethics, there are a few key considerations that one must take into account.

Regardless of the scope or topic of the assessment project in question, take a moment to consider whether the project needs approval from the campus's Institutional Review Board (IRB). IRBs act as a safeguard to ensure that assessment or research projects will not cause any undue harm to their participants. Assessment conducted for normal educational practices (i.e., assessment done in a classroom or to assess a program/service and meant to be used only internally to improve those experiences) is often exempt from IRB review. Nevertheless, it is important to educate oneself about IRB requirements. Campuses typically provide some kind of education and/or training opportunities to staff and faculty to help ensure that the appropriate processes are followed. When dealing with the IRB review process and approval, it is definitely better to be safe than sorry. IRBs are governed by regulations set forth by the U.S. Department of Health and Human Services and violations can carry strict penalties. IRBs are sometimes also referred to as Human Subjects Review Boards.

In addition, it is important to be ethical in how one utilizes the data that are collected even when the assessment is exempt from IRB review. Data that can be traced back to individual students must be treated with respect. Individually identifiable information should never be released publicly and every effort possible should be made to ensure confidentiality (Palomba & Banta, 1999). Furthermore, one should never hide "bad" or "negative" assessment results. It is important to assess programs and services honestly so that less-than-desirable results can be used to inform future improvements and demonstrate progress.

Organizational Politics and Influence

When we think of organizational politics (sometimes referred to as workplace politics or office politics), organizations or entities such as banks or Wall Street may come to mind. Further down the list may or may not be institutions of higher education, but, like any organization, they are not immune to the power play of organizational politics. In higher education institutions, everyone plays a role in organizational politics regardless of whether one is located in academic affairs, student affairs, or business management. Power struggles between actors most commonly emerge over resources. A student affairs staff member attempting to assess a program may find himself or herself in the middle of not only a struggle to obtain resources but also a struggle to maintain control of his or her stated methods and objectives.

Organizational politics is "the management of influence to obtain ends" (Mayer & Allen, 1977, p. 675). Regardless of whether you are a director, vice president, faculty member, or full- or part-time professional, when pursuing an assessment project, you may notice "multiple hands in the popcorn bowl," or better yet, it may begin to feel as if the project is being influenced to take a different route than originally planned.

Organizational politics is defined by influence. Three possible forms of influence that a staff or faculty member may encounter are presented next.

Legitimate Power

Upon beginning a research or assessment project, an actor may find that his or her supervisor, or a superior in the hierarchy of the institution, recommends or hints toward certain outcomes or certain methods to be used when conducting the project. In this case, the actor may not have much of a choice other than to divert resources and make adjustments to the methods.

One of the best ways to prepare and minimize *legitimate power* influence is to include the source of the influence in the process. You must attempt to remain in control by clearly providing your objectives and methods, by explaining where resources will come from and how those resources will be used. Providing a supervisor with the knowledge that any findings are for assessment purposes, to create a more efficient and productive environment, may alleviate his or her concerns.

Rewards

Rewards stem from both vertical and horizontal actors. A person with legitimate power may have the power to positively or negatively reward one's work; however, legitimate power holders do not exclusively control rewards. Positive rewards usually include an increase in resources or acknowledgment, whereas negative rewards are the opposite.

A powerful tool for dealing with actors who wield reward influence is figuring out how you will get and use all necessary resources for your assessment project. In addition to monetary resources, personnel resources, and software/data collection and analysis resources, one of the most valuable resources for assessment projects is time. Remain cognizant of the amount of time the project will take and how it will be spent, and try to plan for contingencies. A powerful tool in the reward influencer's tool chest is the ability to add or take away time that a project needs.

Expert Influence

When working in academia, people tend to gain very specialized skills and knowledge specific to their job responsibilities. Whether these people are on the assessment project team or not, people with control over information wield a great deal of influence. The flow of information presented by an expert can lead to utilization of the most effective methods. However, experts may also shirk their responsibilities to the team and objectives of the study and attempt to divert resources to other objectives, focusing on those particular objectives that more closely resemble their interests.

Strong leadership, planning, and team reflection are needed to counter expert influence as well as to prevent it. Planning the objectives and purpose of the assessment project needs to be a key factor in the assessment process. Continuous reflection on the objectives will allow all actors involved to assess how well the project is adhering to its purpose. Any diversion away from the purpose of the project would be brought to the attention of the group and resolved.

Conclusion

We have described the criteria, resources available, and types of information you should seek to gather in selecting an assessment method. In addition, we have carefully discussed the four key questions you must answer when selecting a method via the Selecting a Method Decision-Making Grid. Furthermore, we have offered descriptions of different types of assessment methods, along with additional considerations such as ethics, organizational politics, and influences. Using these tools and ideas you can thoughtfully and purposely choose the assessment that is right for your task at hand.

References

Banta, T. W., Jones, E. A., & Black, K. E. (2009). *Designing effective assessment: Principles and profiles of good practice.* San Francisco, CA: Jossey-Bass.

Bresciani, M. J., Moore Gardner, M., & Hickmott, J. (2009). *Demonstrating student success: A practical guide to outcomes-based assessment of learning and development in student affairs.* Sterling, VA: Stylus.

Brown, R. M. (1984). *Sudden death.* New York, NY: Bantam Books.

Cohen, A. M., & Brawer, F. B. (2008). *The American community college* (5th ed.). San Francisco, CA: Jossey-Bass.

Mayer, B. T., & Allen, R. W. (1977). Toward a definition of organizational politics. *The Academy of Management Review, 2*(4), 672–678.

Middaugh, M. F. (2010). *Planning and assessment in higher education: Demonstrating institutional effectiveness.* San Francisco, CA: Jossey-Bass.

Palomba, C. A., & Banta, T. W. (1999). *Assessment essentials: Planning, implementing, and improving assessment in higher education.* San Francisco, CA: Jossey-Bass.

Schuh, J. H., Upcraft, M. L., & Associates. (2001). *Assessment practice in student affairs: An applications manual.* San Francisco, CA: Jossey-Bass.

6

ANALYZING AND INTERPRETING RESULTS

Kimberly A. Kline, Joy Battison, and Booker T. Piper, Jr.

The purpose of this chapter is to address the analysis and interpretation of data collected for community and two-year college assessment so that findings can be applied purposely, effectively, and in the proper context. We provide ways to systematically develop procedures for collecting and organizing data, analysis processes, and data interpretation. O'Leary (2005) notes, "Analysis should be approached as a critical, reflective, and iterative process that cycles between data and an overarching research framework that keeps the big picture in mind" (p. 4). The information we provide can be applied to the various levels of assessment that take place at community and two-year colleges, which tend to serve a broader and more diverse population than four-year colleges and universities (Banta, Jones, & Black, 2009).

Being Purposeful and Effective in Data Analysis

When considering a data collection method it is important to keep in mind the mission, goals, and objectives of the research project (Office of Institutional Research & Assessment, 2012). To ensure that the data collected will be valuable to the institution, it is essential to align the assessment and research goals with the mission and vision of the funding institution. This is especially true for projects with community and two-year colleges because their mission statements are designed to define the "physical, social, fiscal, and political contexts in which the institution exists" since they typically serve a more diverse population (Abelman & Dalessandro, 2008, p. 308). The mission statement is a key tool because any assessment performed should be used as a means to improve institutional effectiveness and the mission statement can serve as a road map toward this goal.

It is critical to develop a clearly defined purpose in the beginning stages of an assessment plan. The purpose of the plan will shape decisions that affect the assessment process, such as research collection methods, approaches to data collection, and evaluation of the data. The purpose should be tied not only to the mission of the institution but also to the goals and values of the area the assessment is intended to improve. Throughout each stage of planning, it is important to involve faculty, community representatives, stakeholders, and any other persons who may be affected by the assessment process. If professionals involved collaborate from the onset of the project it will help define the purpose of the assessment, the intended execution strategy, and intended outcomes. This collaboration will curtail the amount of time and resources that may otherwise be spent needlessly and minimize unorganized, directionless data collection (Palomba & Banta, 1999; Servan, 2004).

After an effective assessment plan is in place, the best method of data collection can be determined. Assessment practitioners must decide whether the method of inquiry should be qualitative, quantitative, or mixed. It can be useful to utilize a set of criteria to ensure that you ask similar and equal questions regardless of type. The following five criteria have proven effective in our work when organizing and interpreting data (International Center for Alcohol Practices, 2013):

1. *Relevance:* Does the assessment address an existing need? (Were the outcomes achieved aligned with current priorities? Are we asking the right questions?)
2. *Effectiveness:* Did the assessment achieve the intended outcomes?
3. *Efficiency:* Did the intervention achieve maximum results with available resources?
4. *Results/impact:* Have any changes been implemented as a result of the findings of this assessment in an effort to improve learning or development?
5. *Sustainability:* Can improvements in learning or development last, and will they have far-reaching implications for a student's life as a citizen after college?

Assessment should always be conducted with improved student outcomes in mind; this is especially important at community colleges. As educators, we work at figuring out how students learn, develop, and, at times, serve, and are continually tweaking the ways we interface with them to make the most impact. Assessment is not always a clear-cut process. There are times when it is more important to quickly garner needed information to make responsible decisions to help our students than to complete a detailed research study. The assessment process can provide this type of information if you keep this goal in mind and use the aforementioned criteria as a guide.

It is the job of community college higher education professionals to bring the data collected at a given institution to life. This can be accomplished by thoughtfully interpreting the data keeping in mind the students they serve. Patton (2009) notes, "Data interpretation and analysis involve making sense out of what people have said, looking for patterns, putting together what is said in one place with what is said in another place, and integrating what different people have said" (p. 347).

Describing the Data

Many texts on research methods devote several pages to describing in detail what data are, how they are used, and how they can be interpreted. We believe, however, there are some key facts to keep in mind that can help with assessment analysis, whether simple or very complex. Simply put, data are distinguished in two ways: (a) by their cause and/or effect (dependent and independent variables, respectively), and (b) by the scale of measurement with which they are associated. A variable is any characteristic, number, or quantity that can be measured. An independent variable is not changed by other variables you are trying to measure (e.g., a person's age), while a dependent variable depends on other factors (e.g., if a scientist studies the impact of a drug on cancer, the independent variable is the administration of the drug and the dependent variable is the impact the drug has on cancer).

When we are talking about data in terms of assessment, we are most always describing pieces of information regarding a population or sample (a subset of a population). In social science research, we use the term *statistic* to provide a numerical description of different facets of a population. There are two main types of statistics. *Descriptive statistics* are used to summarize some basic information about the sample, often presented visually through illustrations such as a bar graph or pie chart (O'Leary, 2005).

A second type of statistics, inferential statistics, is used to estimate the degree of confidence that can be placed in generalizations from a sample to a population. Conclusions are drawn based on mathematical probability theory (Rose & Sullivan, 1996). Generally, when research is conducted, it is impossible to contact all members of that population about participating in the study. In these cases, samples or subsets of populations are selected to help the researcher draw conclusions. When samples are used, there is a level of uncertainty about whether or not the data collected actually reflect the overall population. A community or two-year college may be interested in finding out whether traditional or nontraditional students are more likely to use on-campus resources, such as the library. In this case, the researcher must determine the relationship between the variables—type of student and the use of on-campus resources—and compute the level of significance. VanderStoep and Johnston (2009) state, "The level of significance is the probability that a relationship between variables is *not* real, but rather due to chance factors" (p. 94). Significant findings are those that reach a point at which researchers can declare that the relationship between variables is real and not a factor of chance; typically in social sciences, a probability of error of .05 is considered a significant finding (VanderStoep & Johnston, 2009).

When a dependent variable has two or more independent variables that can explain variations, a bivariate analysis is done; when there are three or more potential independent variables, a multivariate analysis is done to find correlations among variables and how they may interact to impact the dependent variable, and provide important information for other more complex data analysis (Rose & Sullivan, 1996).

Although data analysis will most likely not be your primary job responsibility, it is important to have a basic understanding of statistical language. When selecting the appropriate analysis tool, it is essential to know the nature of your variables, which scale of measurement is best to use, the general shape of the distribution of the variables, and what types of questions you wish to ask of the data. If you have a good idea of what it is you want, you will make this task for the data analysis professional with whom you are working much easier.

A *variable* is a concept (e.g., subjective health) that a respondent assesses; a number or value is assigned to that response. As Rose and Sullivan (1996) explain, "Every variable has four essential parts: (1) a name; (2) some sort of verbal definition; (3) a set of categories; and (4) a procedure for carrying out the sorting" (p. 16). Variables are forms of measurement restricted to a set of rules and procedures that dictate how numerical values attach to them; this allows researchers to *analyze* variances in data (Rose & Sullivan, 1996, p. 16). The types of analysis that researchers can perform with specific variables are determined by the level of measurement. In the social sciences, four levels of measurement are commonly used (Bernard, 2000; Rose & Sullivan, 1996): nominal, ordinal, interval, and ratio. A *nominal* (or categorical) variable is a qualitative measurement whose value is not numerical with each category having equal value. One example of a nominal variable would be a "yes or no" survey question, with the response numerically coded (e.g., *yes* = 1 and *no* = 2) ; these numbers are arbitrary and do not reflect any type of value or scale (Bernard, 2000; Rose & Sullivan, 1996).

The values of *ordinal variables* involve ranking; however, a measurement for the differences in value does not exist. Bernard (2000) uses the American social class system (upper, middle, and lower class) as a prime example of an ordinal variable: "The three classes are, in theory, mutually exclusive and exhaustive. In addition, a person who is labelled 'middle class' is lower in the social class hierarchy than someone labelled 'high class'" (p. 43). Because class ranking affects social status and economic influence, there is a clear difference in the values although the degree of the difference is uncertain (Rose & Sullivan, 1996).

Interval variables have a measurable numeric difference, making this level of measurement strictly quantitative, and an arbitrary zero point exists (e.g., the Fahrenheit temperature scale and an IQ scale), but equal differences (e.g., 20 points) do not necessarily reflect the same magnitude of difference. For example, the difference between 40°F and 20°F is 20 points, but 40°F is not twice as hot as 20°F, nor is 0°F twice as cold as 20°F or four times as cold as 40°F (Bernard, 2000; Rose & Sullivan, 1996).

Ratio variables are similar to interval variables except they have a true zero point, where zero means none of that variable. This is true of temperatures on the Kelvin scale and income. If person A earns $20,000 a year, person B earns $40,000 a year, and person C earns $60,000 a year, the $20,000 difference in income between person A and person B is equal to the difference in income between person B and person C (Bernard, 2000; Rose & Sullivan, 1996); however, the differences still have different meanings—as you can see, person A earns half as much as person B, but person B does not earn half as much as person C.

Measures of Central Tendency: Mean, Median, and Mode

Measures of central tendency are used to describe different types of the central value in a frequency distribution (Rose & Sullivan, 1996). The most frequently used measure of central tendency is the mean. The mean represents the average of a set of numbers and can be used to determine, for example, the average number of students in each academic program. To determine the mean, you add all of the numeric code values (e.g., 1 = *yes*; 2 = *no*; 3 = *maybe*) and divide by the total number of subjects (Rose & Sullivan, 1996; Vander-Stoep & Johnston, 2009). The mean may not always be the best approach when determining central tendency. If trying to determine GPA, for example, the median may provide a better representation. The median describes the

Figure 6.1 Median when number of scores is an odd number.

Criminal Justice Students – GPA
1.0, 1.7, 1.9, 2.1, 2.3, 2.5, 2.6, **2.6**, 2.7, 3.2, 3.3, 3.3, 3.3, 3.8, 4.0

Figure 6.2 Median when number of scores is an even number.

Criminal Justice Students – GPA
1.0, 1.7, 1.9, 2.1, 2.3, 2.5, 2.6, **2.6**, **2.7**, 3.2, 3.3, 3.3, 3.3, 3.5, 3.8, 4.0

middle position in the data set (the same number of values above and below). To determine the median GPA for criminal justice students, for example, the data must first be placed in either ascending or descending order. In the example in Figure 6.1, the number of scores is an odd number and the median is the middle score of 2.6. If we were to add another score, making our number of scores an even number, the median would be determined by the average of the two middle scores. In the example in Figure 6.2, the median score would be the average of 2.6 and 2.7, which is 2.65.

The final measure of central tendency is mode. Mode is the score that represents the most frequently occurring score in the distribution. In Figures 6.1 and 6.2, the most frequently occurring score, thus the mode, is 3.3 (Rose & Sullivan, 1996; VanderStoep & Johnston, 2009).

As a result of the qualitative nature of ordinal measures, only median and mode can be used as measures of central tendency. Mean, median, and mode can be used for interval measures as measures of central tendency because of the quantitative nature of these variables. When deciding which measure of central tendency is the most appropriate, the researcher must take into account their data. Generally, mean is used for interval measures and median for ordinal, but when data are highly skewed this is not always suitable. When analyzing interval values in which the distribution is skewed, it may be more ideal to use median as a measure of central tendency (Rose & Sullivan, 1996). For some variables, mean, median, and mode can all be meaningful.

Distribution: Variance and Standard Deviation

Although measures of central tendency give researchers a good starting point in their analysis of data, measuring variations allows researchers to dig deeper. A symmetrical distribution exists when the mean, median, and mode exist at the same point in a distribution; however, this is unusual. More commonly, a distribution will be skewed and will not have a similar mean, median, and mode with the frequencies unevenly distributed to the right or left of center. In a positively skewed distribution, the frequencies are skewed to the right; in a negatively skewed distribution, the frequencies are skewed to the left (Rose & Sullivan, 1996).

Another method that allows researchers to gain more information from their data is measuring the degree of dispersion or *variance* around the mean. This method shows researchers how variables are distributed. A small variance indicates that the variables are close to the mean, whereas a greater variance reveals a broader distribution. Standard deviation is one method that measures the level of dispersion from the mean. If incoming students are required to take an entrance examination prior to signing up for courses, a college may want to compare individuals in the incoming class of students by looking at the standard deviation of scores in that class for different placement tests. The college also may want to compare these scores against the mean of the scores of all students who have previously taken the examination in order to draw various conclusions about the incoming class based on these test scores.

Quantitative Data

Quantitative data collection occurs when the results of assessment are intended to be expressed numerically. According to the Student Affairs Assessment Council (SAAC, 2011), this method is used to represent results through "statistical analysis, description of trends, comparison of groups, relationships among variables, and a comparison of results" (p. 10). Quantitative methods are generally the preferred choice of data collection when sample size is large. Using quantitative methods, researchers are not overwhelmed by the large amounts of textual information that would result from a large-group analysis of qualitative data.

During the development of the quantitative assessment method, objective scoring procedures are used to assign a number to participants' responses that can be entered into data analysis software such as SPSS (Statistical Package for the Social Sciences) (Choban et al., 2004; Schuh, 2009). Sometimes data will have already been formatted for SPSS, Microsoft Excel, or other computerized analysis software; other times, however, data must be manually entered into a computer. All data need to be coded and cleaned (Schuh, 2009) to ensure that all of the data values are entered into the software correctly and that all values are legitimate (e.g., no eights in the data if there is no corresponding value for an eight). Because it can be time-consuming, researchers may wish to have other staff or students help enter the information into a computer software program and clean it; however, the researcher is ultimately responsible if the data are not properly cleaned.

Schuh (2009) suggests several techniques to help during the data coding and entering process. When coding, make sure all data values are uniform in each question; for example, in a Likert-scale survey in which 1 = *strongly disagree* and 5 = *strongly agree*, you will need to make sure that the data values are the same even if the type of scale is different (e.g., an agreement scale to a satisfaction scale). Missing, blank, not applicable, and illogical data must be coded uniformly as well; each should be distinguishable because they do not represent the same response (e.g., a missing value is different from not applicable or does not apply). Lastly, Schuh recommends that both an electronic and a hard-copy codebook of any coding decisions be kept and regularly maintained.

Once you clean and code your data, we recommend you seek out your institutional research director or the point person within your division who typically analyzes data. That person will help you select the appropriate statistical tests based on the nature of your variables, the scales of measurement, the distribution, and, most important, the type of question or questions you asked, and ultimately conduct the analyses.

Qualitative Data

Qualitative or narrative data collection takes place when the intent is to express the voice of the participants through descriptive and holistic narrative concepts rather than through numbers (Choban et al., 2004). This method utilizes distinctive data collection methods including but not limited to observations, carefully shaped open-ended questions, fieldwork, focus groups, and literary text reviews. Typically this assessment method is utilized for smaller groups of informed participants because the data collected are intended to provide in-depth information and include a wide range of responses (Choban et al., 2004; Johnson, Dunlap, & Benoit, 2010; SAAC, 2011). The information attained during the assessment process is descriptive; detailed opinions and perspectives are commonly grouped into repetitive themes that assessment practitioners must analyze to make informed conclusions (Palomba & Banta, 1999). Qualitative data can often be difficult to analyze because it may be viewed as a chaotic "mountain of words" that is seen as lacking the structure of quantitative data (Dunlap & Benoit, 2010; Office of Institutional Research & Assessment, 2012). Therefore, it is especially important to keep the data organized from the onset of the research project.

There are a number of different approaches to collecting and organizing qualitative data. Schuh (2009) created a three-step process for assessment practitioners to develop and implement data plans effectively: "Consideration should be given to (1) data collection methods that align with the purpose and objectives of the assessment, (2) how different methods of data collection are implemented and carried out, and (3) advantages and challenges of using various data collection methods" (p. 52). For example, if the purpose of an assessment is to determine whether students at a community college are satisfied with the on-campus housing that is currently provided, a locally developed web-based questionnaire would be an appropriate inquiry method. On the other hand, if the purpose is to determine *why* students are satisfied or not satisfied with current housing, a focus group would be an appropriate inquiry method.

Interpreting the Data

For data analysis to be effective, researchers must stay focused on the primary goals of the data collection. Regardless of the type of data being analyzed, data management involves

- familiarizing yourself with appropriate software;
- developing a data management system;
- systematically organizing and screening your data;
- entering the data into a program; and finally,
- "cleaning" your data. (O'Leary, 2005)

Computer Software

Remember that being able to conduct statistical analysis no longer means being able to work with mathematical formulas. It is more important to be able to learn the language and logic of applied statistics and assessment. Being competent in the use of statistical software that has been developed for the social sciences such as SPSS for quantitative data and NVivo and NUD*IST for qualitative data will help you stand out among your peers. For many years, social scientists rated SPSS as the number one choice for a statistical programming package. The program was invented by a social scientist and appealed to practitioners in the field because the program was designed specifically to analyze quantitative data using descriptive statistics, tabulation, multivariate analysis, ratios, and bivariate statistics. In the beginning, one of the appeals of using SPSS was the excellent manual that supported the program; however, later editions of the manual for the program are not considered as user friendly and use of SPSS has fallen.

NVivo and NUD*IST are two research analysis computer software programs that have been designed to allow you to collect and analyze qualitative and mixed-methods data. Originally NUD*IST, specifically NUD*IST 6, broke new ground in that it allowed the researcher to analyze large amounts of narrative data at once. It is worth mentioning that our team had difficulty choosing between NVivo and NUD*IST. Ultimately, we found the following information provided by QSR International (2013), the parent company of both NUD*IST and NVivo, to be useful: "Our NVivo 10 software supersedes N6. It includes the features of N6 and much more—including the ability to work with PDFs, surveys, web and social media data, photos, video and audio files. NVivo 10 also allows you to open and work with projects you've developed in N6." In addition, QSR is a Microsoft partner and developed its interface similarly to Microsoft so that it is recognizable to its users. It also allows users to work in multiple languages to allow information to be shared globally.

It is important for researchers to choose software that will organize and analyze their research in the most efficient way possible. When selecting a program it is essential that you, as a scholarly professional, have a basic understanding of both qualitative and quantitative analysis and the terminology associated with each methodology.

Presenting Your Data Findings

Your findings and conclusions must, of course, accurately reflect the data. They need to be coherent and presented in a way that speaks to the group you are addressing and show clearly the relevance of your project (O'Leary, 2005). Findings should be placed in the context of the current peer-reviewed research on the topic or problem, stressing their applicability to the overall learning outcomes for your program, department, division, or institution; you also need to present the limitations of your study. As mentioned earlier, assessment is often not designed to be generalizable to a larger population outside your institution. The more you work in the area of data collection, the more comfortable you will become in discerning whether a study is generalizable or not: Is it an assessment project or a full research study? Though not exhaustive, in this section we attempt to provide you with basic criteria to consider while preparing your date findings for dissemination to various stakeholders within the college/university system.

Evidence

It is not always necessary to conduct an extensive research study in order to learn valuable information on how to support student success. It is important to ensure that your campus has a comprehensive understanding of how assessment provides evidence on student learning and development (SAAC, 2011). Evidence can be used to foster the progression on a campus by

- encouraging informed decision making,
- evaluating the success of existing programs and services on campus,
- revealing programs and services that have not been successful or that might benefit from more support,
- demonstrating the need to conduct larger research projects, and
- supplying data for learning outcomes.

Association

An association or correlation exists if the occurrence of one variable is affected by the presence, absence, or score of another event (variable). If the relationship between the two variables is positive, an increase in one variable will cause an increase in the other; if their relationship is negative, a decrease in one will cause an increase in the other.

Causation

Typically when we think of the word *causation* in social science research we define it as "a: the act or process of causing [or] b: the act or agency which produces an effect" (www.merriam-webster.com). From a validity and reliability standpoint, causation is vitally important to our work because it allows for a direct explanation of how one variable impacts another. The alternative, correlation, only allows us to say the two variables are related in some way (e.g., being able to say height has a positive impact on income versus having to say that being tall is correlated with higher income). Results that can reflect causality are much more important in that they can help shape policies and programs that will be more effective. This is important not only to the scientific community, but also for the stakeholders who have funded the research.

Reliability

Reliability demonstrates the level of consistency: Multiple measures of the same concept should yield the same result. For example, if a community college applicant is required to take a proficiency exam in math prior to being placed in college courses, if the exam has high reliability the student should have similar results if he or she were to take the exam more than once. However, reliability does not measure the level of validity of a measurement. Using the math exam, if the student's score on the exam did not represent his or her knowledge of math, it would not be valid no matter how reliable it was.

Reliability can be assessed in several ways. Treiman (2009) suggests the following three methods to measure the reliability of a scale:

1. Test-retest reliability: the correlation of two results taken at separate times
2. Alternate-forms reliability: the correlation of two different tests that measure the same outcome
3. Internal-consistency reliability: the correlation between the different items that make up a scale (p. 244)

Validity

Validity evaluates the accuracy of measuring the intended concept. If a student is required to take a math entrance exam in order to be admitted to a community college, this exam should have a logical connection between the purpose (assessment of college math skills) and its indicators (the exam questions). The entrance exam would have high validity if it asked students to solve mathematical questions at an appropriate difficulty level to show understanding of college-level mathematics.

Validity and reliability are focused on ensuring the quality of measurements. These concepts, however, are not necessarily interdependent. A measurement may be reliable but not valid; however, if a measurement is highly unreliable it cannot be valid (Rose & Sullivan, 1996, p. 246).

Stakeholders in Community College Assessment

More than any other type of institution, community and two-year colleges have stakeholders present in their immediate neighborhood, along with those stakeholders at both the county and state level. Although it is important to involve representatives from each of these groups, it is strategic to involve representatives in specific areas of assessment within which they have the most expertise. For instance, stakeholders from Ford Motor Company may be interested in the course- and program-level outcomes of a community college graduate being trained to work within a specific operation at Ford, a major employer for the area. Stakeholders at the state level, however, may be more interested in institutional-level student learning outcomes for employment in many areas in the state's economy as well as how well students are being prepared for service as community leaders. Whatever the priority of a given stakeholder, we suggest utilizing a set of questions developed by Bresciani, Moore Gardner, and Hickmott (2009) when designing each step of the outcomes-based assessment process:

1. What individuals, groups, offices, or departments might be affected by the outcomes-based assessment process?
2. How might representatives from such groups contribute to the outcomes-based assessment process?
3. What other stakeholders can we partner with to develop and implement an effective outcomes-based assessment process?
4. What resources are available to promote and secure acceptance and involvement by stakeholders?
5. What resources and insights might our stakeholders provide for the outcomes-based assessment process?
6. What is the best use of stakeholder time and talent during the outcomes-based assessment process, and how can we maximize the use of each? (pp. 72–73)

Utilizing these questions will lead to a more surgical and granular approach to managing the outcomes-based assessment process for community and two-year colleges, as well as encourage involvement that has meaning to the stakeholders.

Thoughts on Stakes-Based Assessment

Because this chapter is dealing with the ways in which we interpret and analyze assessment data, it is very important to consider the conditions under which the assessments being conducted take place. The congruency that at one time existed between the level of risk or stakes that were present at the time of an assessment and the level of risk or stakes of how that information was interpreted is now virtually nonexistent. In fact, many low-stakes testing situations for placement of the college-going public, for instance, in a community or two-year college now may have a high-stakes impact on funding for that institution, and how the college is perceived by stakeholders. Because of the level of accountability now expected in some states for community and two-year colleges, it is imperative that we as shepherds of these data understand exactly what low-, middle-, and high-stakes assessment mean and the impact these types of assessments have on our students and the campus community. According to Barry and Finney (2009), "Oftentimes the measures given in order to make high stakes decisions about program effectiveness have relatively little personal meaning or importance to the students completing them" (p. 1).

Low-stakes testing or assessment occurs when the individual involved in the assessment has no connection or vested interest in the outcome of (a) their answers to the assessment or (b) the implications of the results for the college or university as a whole. Furthermore, because the data generated are based on self-report, there is a risk of low levels of validity for reporting purposes, although the data are useful when analyzed and interpreted in combination with other forms of assessment.

An example of high-stakes testing or assessment is when the failure to achieve a high grade will have a direct and significant consequence for a student (e.g., failing a comprehensive exam as a political science major in a student's senior year will prohibit the student from graduating with a baccalaureate degree in political science). When used correctly, both low- and high-stakes testing can play an important role in giving us valuable information about how our students learn, develop lifelong skills such as empathy, and care about particular social issues that impact all of our communities. For instance, low-stakes testing can help pinpoint deficiencies in the level of preparedness in specific areas so we can provide students with the tools and support they need to be successful. High-stakes tests can help a school or department identify and correct weaknesses in its programs.

Conclusion

We have discussed ways to analyze and interpret data collected for community and two-year college assessment and provided methods for developing procedures for collecting and organizing data in an effective and purposeful way. It is important to remember that you must keep your eye on the overarching end results desired, manage your data, engage in the actual process of quantitative and/or qualitative analysis, present your data within the appropriate context, and be able to draw meaningful and logical conclusions (O'Leary, 2005).

References

Abelman, R., & Dalessandro, A. (2008). The institutional vision of community colleges: Assessing style as well as substance. *Community College Review, 35*(4), 306–335.

Banta, T. W., Jones, E. A., & Black, K. E. (2009). *Designing effective assessment: Principles and profiles of good practice.* San Francisco, CA: Jossey-Bass.

Barry, C. L., & Finney, S. J. (2009). Does it matter how data are collected? A comparison of testing conditions and the implications for validity. *Research & Practice in Assessment, 3*, 1–15.

Bernard, H. R. (2000). *Social research methods: Qualitative and quantitative approaches.* Thousand Oaks, CA: Sage.

Bresciani, M. J., Moore Gardner, M., & Hickmott, J. (2009). *Demonstrating student success in student affairs.* Sterling, VA: Stylus Publishing.

Choban, G. C., Edwards, R., Eisenberg, H., Fenn, P., Godwin, J., Haney, P., & Wilson, C. (2004). An assessment framework for the community college: Measuring student learning and achievement as a means of demonstrating institutional effectiveness. *League, 1*, 1–35.

Dunlap & Benoit, 2010 International Center for Alcohol Practices. (2013). *Data analysis and interpretation.* Retrieved from http://www.icap.org/Policy Tools/Toolkits/EvaluationToolkit/4DataAnalysisandInterpretation/tabid/446/ Default.aspx

International Center for Alcohol Policies. (2013). Data analysis and interpretation. Retrieved from http://www.icap.org/PolicyTools/Toolkits/EvaluationToolkit/4D ataAnalysisandInterpretation/tabid/446/Default.aspx

Johnson, B. D., Dunlap, E., & Benoit, E. (2010). Organizing "mountains of words" for data analysis, both qualitative and quantitative. *Substance Use & Misuse, 45*(5), 648–670.

Office of Institutional Research & Assessment. (2012). *Analyzing and interpreting data.* Retrieved from https:oira.syr.edu/assessment/assesspp/analyze.htm

O'Leary, Z. (2005). Analysing and interpreting data. [PowerPoint slides]. Retrieved from www.uk.sagepub.com/resources/oleary2/ch11.ppt

Palomba, C. A., & Banta, T. W. (1999). *Assessment essentials: Planning, implementing, and improving assessment in higher education.* San Francisco, CA: Jossey-Bass.

Patton, L. (2009). My sister's keeper: A qualitative examination of mentoring experiences among African American women in graduate and professional schools. *The Journal of Higher Education, 80*(5), 510–537.

QSR International. (2013). *Products.* Retrieved from http://www.qsrinternational .com/products_previous-products_n6.aspx

Rose, D., & Sullivan, O. (1996). *Introducing data analysis for social scientists.* Philadelphia, PA: Open University Press.

Schuh, J. (2009). *Assessment methods for student affairs.* New York, NY: Wiley & Sons.

Servan, A. M. (2004). Assessment of student learning outcomes at the institutional level. *New Directions for Community College, 2004*(126), 17–27.

Student Affairs Assessment Council (SAAC). (2011). *Assessment handbook: Assessment practice* (pp. 1–18). Portland, OR: Portland State University.

Treiman, D. J. 2009. *Quantitative data analysis: Doing social research to test ideas.* San Francisco: Jossey-Bass/Wiley.

VanderStoep, S. W., & Johnston, D. D. (2009). *Research methods for everyday life: Blending qualitative and quantitative approaches.* San Francisco, CA: Jossey-Bass.

7

USING AND
COMMUNICATING RESULTS

Stephanie Romano and Megan Daane Lawrence

In this chapter we focus on the communication and use of assessment results in a community or two-year college setting. Written through the lens of Heald College, a regionally accredited, private, for-profit two-year institution, we offer a number of strategies to develop and support effective communication practices during the assessment process. Moreover, we introduce and discuss a variety of tools to "close the loop" and offer insights for using the results of assessment to inform accountability measures and enhance student learning development. Finally, we designed this chapter to allow the reader to learn from our assessment "story" in an effort to inform the creation or continuation of effective and sustainable assessment practices and contribute to overall institutional and student success.

Overview of Heald College

Heald College is a private, for-profit school based in San Francisco, California, with 12 campuses in California, Oregon, and Hawai'i, and a central administrative office in San Francisco. Heald was founded in 1863 and holds regional accreditation by the Accrediting Commission for Community and Junior Colleges (ACCJC) of the Western Association of Schools and Colleges (WASC). Heald offers associate's degree, diploma, and certificate programs in health care, technology, and business. It also offers fully online course options for enrolled students, but fully online programs are only in the beginning phases of implementation at the time of this writing.

Heald is geographically dispersed but is accredited as one school. When an instructional program is approved by its accreditor, Heald implements that same program, which might include on-campus and online delivery modalities, consistently at all campus locations. Procedures for designing, developing, and improving instructional programs reflect collaboration with faculty from across the institution. Curriculum managers—who are purposefully not subject matter experts in their discipline but are, rather, expert curriculum designers, program managers, and facilitators— facilitate this collaboration and work with campus instructional program leaders, called program directors, to support the effective implementation of programs and ensure that each campus engages in program review and student learning outcome (SLO) assessment.

Cocurricular programs are provided across all campuses. Procedures that support the effective and efficient implementation of cocurricular programs are developed through collaborative processes facilitated by Central Administrative Office functional leaders. Those procedures are then implemented at each location, though there can be unique elements at each campus.

This distributed and matrixed structure complicates program review and SLO assessment. Practitioners at the campus and online group (collectively referred to in this chapter as the "local" level) need to be able to assess SLOs and identify locally based improvements. At the same time, SLOs are also assessed at an institutional level and some improvements must be made institutionally. Examples of a local improvement would be the upgrading of a piece of equipment in a lab or the addition of a piece of simulation software for online delivery of a course. An example of an institutional improvement would be the modification of a course prerequisite within an instructional program. Heald's institutional effectiveness model take these requirements into account, and the procedures described in this chapter for communicating and using SLO assessment results reflect this complexity.

Establishing a Culture of Safe, Transparent, and Inclusive Communication

Up until 2008, Heald's program review procedures were informal and did not include systematic, institution-wide program review and assessment of SLOs. As the college transitioned to a new model that included faculty and staff from all campuses, online teaching, and in-depth, institutional consideration of teaching and learning, we quickly recognized that this transition would lay bare our day-to-day practices and the effectiveness of teaching and learning at both the local and institutional level. Further, because our planned processes were deeply integrated with strategic planning and budgeting, that raw visibility would extend to the board of trustees.

Understandably, with such intense scrutiny came trepidation, particularly from local administrators, faculty, and staff. Numerous related questions emerged: What happens if our assessment results show that our students are struggling to master SLOs in our program? Will the accreditor prescribe changes? Will the accreditor pull approval for our program? Will my annual evaluation be negatively impacted if I report that students who take my class are struggling to master certain concepts? Will my salary increase be tied to student performance in my classroom? There were also questions that reflected a general skepticism about local and institutional commitment to use SLO data to make meaningful improvements. Heald's institutional administrators considered these questions and reviewed related literature to determine how to respond.

Using assessment results, most specifically using results to drive planning and budgeting, has proven challenging for many institutions (Maki, 2004). This challenge has been somewhat mitigated at Heald by having an institutional effectiveness staff (a group of four who report up to the chief academic officer) support institutional structures and processes for planning, program review, and SLO assessment. Planning, structured to occur at both the central and local level, is informed by the data prepared by the institutional effectiveness staff, which includes assessment of SLO data.

Drawing on best practices in change management and assessment experts, Heald's institutional effectiveness staff determined that it needed to do four things to establish a strong culture of open communication that would allow the college to deeply and honestly engage in program review and assessment:

1. Set expectations about how SLO assessment data would be used and clearly communicate those in writing.
2. Commit to transparency in all aspects of program review, budget procedures, and improvement planning and implementation.
3. Create a culture of safety and open dialogue.
4. Create an inclusive environment where local practitioners play a significant role.

Setting Expectations About the Use of SLO Assessment Data

Nichols and Nichols (2005) describe that the most effective messaging used in best practice assessment institutions combines the need to improve the institution and student learning and the requirements of accrediting agencies. Additionally, the institution's chief executive officer (CEO) has a key role in assuaging concerns that assessment results will not be used for program discontinuance or individual appraisals but rather to drive improvement, and this message is best reinforced verbally with follow-up written communications (Nichols & Nichols, 2005, p. 52).

Heald set the stage for open communications by documenting and training faculty and administrators on how SLO assessment data would and, just as important, would not be used at Heald. The college described how SLO assessment fit into our larger program review and strategic planning processes, how faculty participated in these processes, how decisions were ultimately made as to how improvements would be prioritized and implemented, and how the college would communicate with faculty and administrators throughout.

Leadership found it important to make sure that the initial rollout and related communication was clear, consistent, enthusiastic, and reached all faculty and administrators. This was accomplished by first holding a one-day in-service with program directors and key administrators from all campuses. The college's president and CEO was present for the entire meeting and made opening remarks as to the institution's commitment to program review and SLO assessment. Both his presence and his presentation primed the audience, for he publicly stated, "Though this process is required by our accrediting agency, it is the right thing to do for Heald College" (N. Miura, personal communication, May 1, 2008). The remainder of the in-service was spent describing systematic program review and how the college would be using program review and SLO assessment data to improve the institution, as well as how faculty and administrators would be integrally involved. This one-day in-service was followed up by numerous web conference training sessions and break-out teleconference working sessions with faculty and administrators participating in instructional and cocurricular program review. Heald's president remained actively present in the development and implementation of program review by sending e-mail updates to Heald administrators, staff, and faculty at key milestones. This ongoing presence of the president was vital not only to successfully implementing systematic program review in 2008, but to sustaining those efforts into 2013.

Committing to Transparency

The questions from faculty, staff, and administrators described previously were a key driver in developing communication strategies related to program review and SLO assessment. Local practitioners were skeptical that their data and input would be heard and considered by campus and institutional leadership. Faculty, particularly, were fearful about the ways in which their data would be used. Bresciani, Moore Gardner, and Hickmott (2009) advocate for the transparency of assessment results, and a commitment was made at all levels of the institution to complete transparency to ensure successful results. Suskie (2009) recommended that reports incorporate threshold data wherever possible, and Heald College has adopted that recommendation as well.

If the college expected local practitioners and administrators to be transparent with their SLO data and teaching practices, local and institutional senior administrators at Heald would need to be transparent too. Just as expectations were established regarding the role of program review and SLO assessment, institutional leaders overtly committed to transparency at all levels of the organization with the goal of lifting the veil of mystery from all aspects of program review, budget procedures, and improvement planning and implementation. Further, to demonstrate an institutional commitment to assessment, the college adopted several strategies that Maki (2004) recommends, including calendaring assessment events. Campus administrators made this commitment with the support of executive leadership and then based our future communication decisions and strategies on this fundamental principle.

Creating a Culture of Safety and Open Dialogue

Perhaps the most challenging concern to overcome on our campus was that of safety. Fear of negative repercussions from accreditor and corporate administrators came primarily from program directors and campus administrators. Fears related to the accreditor were addressed by clearly communicating WASC's expectations related to program review and SLO assessment. Institutional communications also demonstrated how corporate administrators and the board fit into the strategic planning and budgeting process so their roles and responsibilities were transparent.

Another major concern that threatened open communication of data and observations was the fear many faculty held about how SLO assessment data would be used in their annual evaluations. But implementation was another matter altogether. The college needed support and commitment at all levels of the institution. After securing the commitment of the president and CEO (Nichols & Nichols, 2005), he wrote to all faculty, campus presidents, regional vice presidents, and the central management team that SLO assessment results would not be used to evaluate faculty or inform promotions or salary considerations. Instead, faculty would be expected to participate in assessment processes, a communication largely modeled after the one recommended by Nichols and Nichols (2005).

This message was reinforced throughout the organization in discussions on the campuses and at the central office. The college was true to this message by ensuring that all SLO data for instructional and cocurricular programs were presented in aggregate at the campus/online level and the overall institutional level. Individuals, such as individual faculty members or individual administrators, were never reflected in the SLO data results that were presented. As added assurance to faculty, user rights in the assessment tracking software, TracDat, were established to ensure that only the college's institutional effectiveness staff (which includes institutional research) could see individual faculty members' SLO assessment entries. All other SLO assessment data were provided through summary reports from the system.

Heald listened intently to the concerns of faculty and staff and addressed them head-on through careful management of access to and communication of SLO assessment results. The college needed the support of and reinforcement from upper management and were successful in obtaining it because of our management's fundamental commitment to institutional effectiveness.

Creating an Inclusive Environment

Heald committed early on to ensure that SLO assessment was an inclusive process that included all levels and all programs—instructional and cocurricular—of the institution. Frameworks that allowed local practitioners, particularly cocurricular staff, dedicated time to participate in assessment (Bresciani et al., 2009) were established. Some student service units even set aside time during annual meetings to engage in and reflect on assessment results. Figure 7.1 depicts the interaction of local practitioners and institutional teams. Although the image references faculty and instructional programs, this conceptual framework can be adapted for cocurricular programs as well.

Figure 7.1 Interaction of local practitioners and institutional teams.

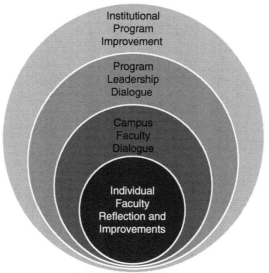

Heald's Integrated Program Review, SLO Assessment, and Strategic Planning

Using assessment results, most specifically using results to drive planning and budgeting, has proven challenging for many institutions (Maki, 2004), and Heald's processes have evolved to create a synchronized integration of SLO assessment, program review, planning, and budgeting, as overseen by the central office's senior director of institutional effectiveness. Originally, strategic planning and institutional effectiveness were overseen by different individuals. When oversight for both processes was combined under the senior director of institutional effectiveness, the college realized improved process integration. Strategic planning was integrated into the assessment management software, and reports were configured to link program review improvements to strategic plans and budget requests. Figure 7.2 provides an overview of the annual cycle and shows where SLO assessment fits within that cycle.

Overview of SLO Assessment Design

Heald uses three types of SLOs: institutional, program, and course:

- Institutional SLOs are SLOs that all students, regardless of program, are expected to master upon completion of an instructional program. An example of an institutional SLO is "Communicates effectively using a variety of methods."
- Instructional program SLOs are program-specific SLOs that students are expected to master upon completion of their degree program. Cocurricular programs also have program SLOs that students are expected to master, such as using the virtual library for research.
- Course SLOs are only in instructional programs and identify the knowledge, skills, and abilities that students are expected to master upon completion of the course.

These SLOs are conceptually designed to answer the question, "Of those persons who use our services, programs, and facilities, is there any effect on their learning, development, [or] academic success?" (Schuh & Associates, 2008, p. 218). All SLOs are developed through dialogue and collaboration between local practitioners and institutional administrators and once established are implemented at all campuses. Course (only for instructional programs), institutional, and program SLOs are listed in the Heald College Academic Catalog. Program SLOs in instructional and cocurricular programs, and course SLOs in instructional programs, are linked to institutional SLOs

Figure 7.2 Integrated planning, program review, and assessment cycles.

Planning, Program Review, and Assessment
Integrated Process Overview

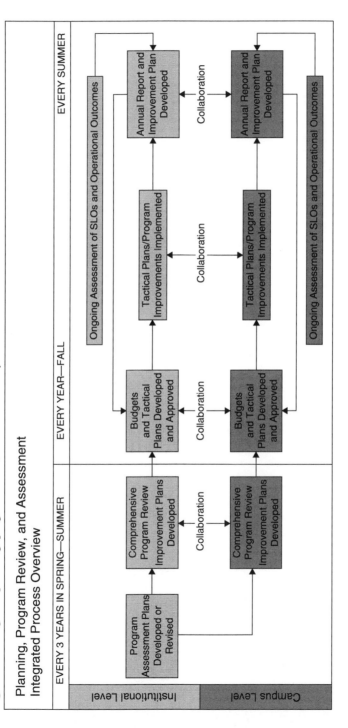

through program outcome maps and are assessed according to the time frames reflected in a program's assessment plan.

Institutional SLOs

Students are given opportunities to develop their mastery of institutional SLOs through general education courses; core courses within our programs; and their experiences with cocurricular programs, such as library services and career services.

Each instructional program is designed to include a culminating experience course, which is either a capstone course or an internship/externship course. Externships are required in health care programs. In non–health care programs, internships are encouraged, and if an internship is not feasible, a student takes a capstone course. The internship or externship experience is an opportunity for students to demonstrate mastery of program and institutional SLOs within a practical workplace setting. Site supervisor evaluations, which were redeveloped to align with program and institutional SLOs, are completed by the site supervisor at the end of a student's internship or externship. Capstone courses, which may be taken in place of an internship, are comprehensive, classroom-based simulations where students can demonstrate mastery of program and institutional SLOs. Capstone projects and corresponding rubrics are developed by faculty and align with program and institutional SLOs.

Site supervisor evaluations and capstone rubric results are collected and used to directly assess students' mastery of both institutional and program SLOs. Program and institutional SLOs are also assessed using indirect methods, including graduate surveys (where available), student internship/externship self-evaluations, and employer surveys.

Institutional SLO data are published annually in the college's Institutional Factbook, which in turn is considered during the college's annual SWOT (strengths, weaknesses, opportunities, and threats) analysis processes. This allows for analysis of institutional learning outcome data at the campus and aggregate level.

Program SLOs

Students are given the opportunity to demonstrate mastery of cocurricular program SLOs at various points during their degree program, depending on when they engage with that particular program. For example, Heald's career services program has a program SLO that students should be able to demonstrate effective interviewing skills. Students demonstrate these skills during mock interviews that typically occur toward the end of the instructional program when the student is preparing to begin job interviews. A rubric that maps to the program SLO is used to ensure consistency of assessment at the local and institutional level.

Students are given the opportunity to demonstrate mastery of instructional program SLOs during the culminating experience course (the internship, externship, or capstone) at the end of their instructional program. As described earlier, internship and externship site supervisor evaluations and capstone rubrics used in these courses align with institutional and program SLOs.

Course SLOs

Course SLOs are published in the Heald College Academic Catalog and in faculty syllabi and are used consistently across Heald, regardless of campus or delivery modality, to guide course content and teaching strategies. Program outcome maps for each program reflect how each course contributes to mastery of program and institutional SLOs.

Students are given the opportunity to demonstrate mastery of course SLOs through embedded benchmark assignments. A benchmark assignment is either an exam or a project with a corresponding rubric. Faculty course development teams, facilitated by institutional curriculum managers, design the benchmark assignment and, where appropriate, a corresponding rubric. These benchmark assignments are then shared with and used by all faculty who teach the course at all campuses. Benchmark assignments are also embedded in online courses to ensure consistency regardless of delivery modality. If a course can be delivered face-to-face and in an online format, a consistent benchmark assignment and, if appropriate, rubric are used for both delivery modalities.

Capturing SLO Data

The results of evaluation forms, rubrics, and exam data used to determine how well students have mastered institutional, program, and course SLOs are captured on an ongoing basis in Heald's assessment system, TracDat. Local practitioners input the results from their classes or student activity, and these results are then aggregated through TracDat to identify trends at the institutional level.

Because SLO data are captured at the local level, faculty and local practitioners in cocurricular programs can reflect on their own practices and make improvements on an ongoing basis. In keeping with our commitment to safety in the SLO assessment process, reports from TracDat are limited to aggregated results. Individual data cannot be tracked back to the specific individual practitioner by individuals outside of the institutional effectiveness staff. Figure 7.3 shows an example of local data, specifically what an individual faculty member would input for a course rubric.

Figure 7.3 Example of local SLO data.

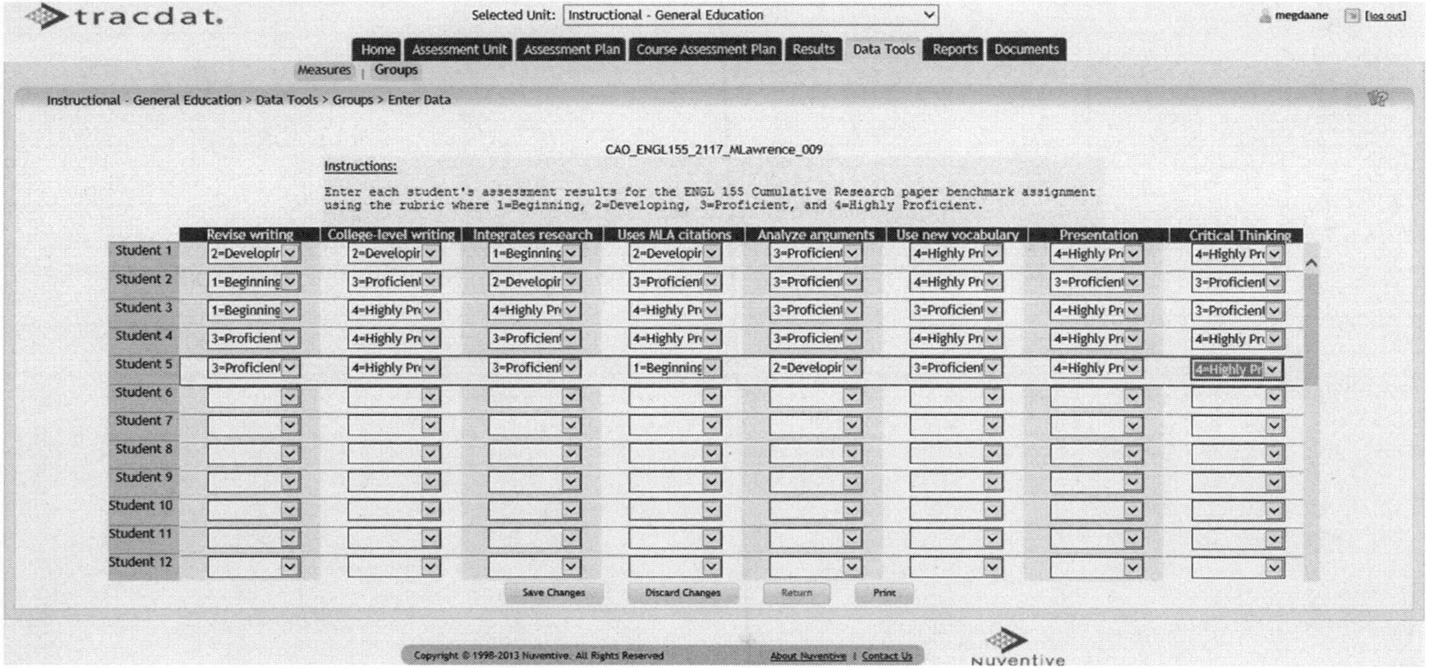

SLO Assessment

SLO data are used to assess SLOs and identify opportunities for improvement. SLO data assessment is conducted at the local and institutional level. This strategy honors the complexity of our matrixed institution and allows for local reflection of results and locally developed improvements as well as institutional reflection and development of improvements.

Local Dialogue

SLO results for instructional programs at the local level are aggregated and shared at the campus or with the online group to facilitate dialogue about student learning trends faculty are seeing on their campuses. Figure 7.4 is

Figure 7.4 Excerpt of report generated by institutional effectiveness group using TracDat data.

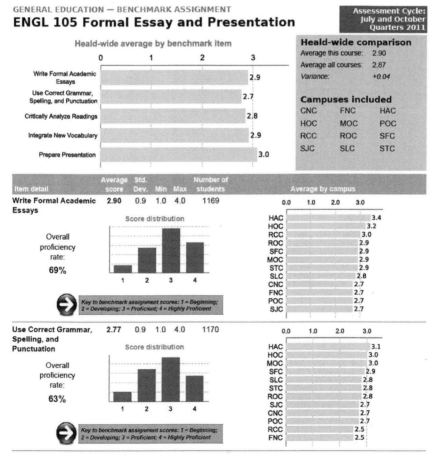

an example of a report that would be generated by the college's institutional effectiveness staff using the assessment data that faculty have entered into TracDat. A report like this is provided to local program leadership and faculty.

Institutional staff prepare the reports, probing questions, and other supporting material for each campus and, for online courses, the online academic leadership. Using this type of report, local practitioners at each campus or with the online group engage in dialogue to understand what the results show, what the root causes might be of the positive, flat, or negative trends in student learning as reflected in the data. Together these teams identify improvements that could lead to enhanced student learning. This dialogue occurs during an event called "Assessment Palooza," a name chosen to deliberately invoke a sense of joy around the celebration of SLO assessment. Such "celebrations" of assessment are important for increasing buy-in and overall engagement among faculty and administrators (Bresciani et al., 2009). Figure 7.5 presents a sample of a local Assessment Palooza agenda.

After Assessment Palooza, lead faculty from each campus and online faculty prepare an outcome assessment record (see Figure 7.6), modeled after that proposed by Nichols and Nichols (2005). This outcome assessment

Figure 7.5 Sample local Assessment Palooza agenda.

Agenda

I. Opening Comments
   a. Introductions
   b. Background—What is Palooza?
   c. Objective—What is our goal?
   d. Principles of Dialogue
II. Palooza Assessment Overview
III. Overview of Assessment Data Packet of Materials
   a. Benchmark Assignment for each course
   b. Benchmark Rubric for each assignment
   c. Data for each campus average of SLOs
   d. Separate documents
   e. Data for each course across campuses—"Palooza Campus Course Average_06042012"
   f. SMART Goals handout
   g. Blank outcome assessment record template (for PD only)
IV. Discussion of Course Families
V. Break
VI. Overview of SMART Goals
VII. Action Plans
VIII. Wrap-Up

Figure 7.6 Example of a blank outcome assessment record.

Outcome Assessment Record

Program Name	
Submission Date	
Submitted By	

From the Assessment Plan *(will be pro-populated in TracDat)*	
Outcome:	
Assessment Method:	
Standard of Success:	

Result: *(What did the data show? What were the trends? What may be causing this trend? What are some solutions to improve this outcome?)*

Result Type:
□ Benchmarking
□ Inconclusive
□ Standard Met
□ Standard Not Met

Action Plan Status
□ Action Complete
□ Action Not Approved
□ Action Plan In Progress
□ No Action Required

record is then recorded in TracDat. Figure 7.7 presents an excerpt of a Trac-Dat report with results of campus-level SLO assessment and related actions. These assessment record reports are generated and posted on Heald's institutional effectiveness intranet site. This increases transparency and offers yet another avenue of communication during the assessment process.

Cocurricular programs collect their assessment data in very similar ways. Because of the nature of the activity of these departments, new constructs, such as Assessment Palooza, are not necessarily needed to support their dialogue. Rather, SLO assessment activities and the development of the outcome assessment record often occur during regularly scheduled staff meetings.

Institutional Dialogue

Cocurricular programs hold cross-campus meetings to discuss institutional SLO data. These meetings are facilitated by the institutional functional leader. Institutional improvements are identified, and local improvements are further refined through this dialogue. An outcome assessment record reflecting institutional assessment results is developed and shared with the cocurricular local practitioners through the institutional effectiveness intranet site.

Figure 7.7 Excerpt of a TracDat report.

Unit Course Assessment Report— Four Column

Heald College

Instructional — General Education

Statement of Purpose: The General Education program supports the institutional mission of preparing students for academic, personal, and professional success by expanding their understanding of the world and cultures around them, fostering a spirit of inquiry, and providing development of their skills, knowledge, and intellectual habits.

Major topics of the program include communication skills, computational skills, social science, natural science, and humanities/fine arts.

Upon successful completion of the general education component of the program of study, students will be able to demonstrate literacy, critical thinking, personal and social responsibility, and resource proficiency.

Additionally, the program outcomes and topics support students who wish to transfer credit upongraduation from Heald.

Course Outcomes	Means of Assessment & Standards of Success/Tasks	Results	Action & Follow-Up
Instructional – General Education – ENGL 105 – Composition and Reading – SLO's 1. Write formal, academic essays 2. Use correct grammar, spelling, and punctuation when writing 3. Critically analyze readings 4. Integrate new vocabulary in writing 5. Prepare presentation(s) using principles of organization and formal language (Created By Instructional – General Education) **Assessment Years:** 2011 **Course Outcome Status:** Active	**Assessment Method:** Benchmark Assignment: Formal Essay and Presentation **Standard of Success:** Aggregate campus average of 3.0 out of 4.0 or better	08/08/2013 – Campus average – 2.8 The class focused on difference material than the Benchmark. Inconsistent delivery of Benchmark. **Result Type:** Inconclusive **Campus:** CNC **Participants (Include Titles):** Instructors: Sanjay Suri, Miranda Smith, Harry Barnes, and Serina Vizzini; Program Director: Marcia Robinson	08/02/2012 – Include more analytical skills such as developing a thesis and topic sentence. **Priority:** 1 – High **Target Completion Date:** 08/01/2013 08/02/2012 – Remove critically analyzing readings. **Priority:** 1 – High **Target Completion Date:** 08/01/2013 08/02/2013 – Align Benchmark with course material; analysis versus writing

Institutional dialogue on instructional program SLO assessment occurs during institutional Assessment Paloozas. These Assessment Paloozas are attended by the lead faculty for each instructional program from each campus and from the online group. Program faculty teams are provided with their program's aggregate SLO data reports and dialogue over the results. Each faculty member is expected to bring forward the insights and recommended improvements from his or her local Assessment Palooza. Each program's curriculum manager facilitates and takes notes for the program faculty team's cross-campus discussion of assessment results.

The results of this cross-campus faculty dialogue are reflected in an outcome assessment record, as shown earlier for campus-level assessment, which is then recorded in TracDat. In keeping with our commitment to transparency, Heald publishes these records as reports on its institutional effectiveness intranet site, where it is available to all Heald staff and faculty.

Using SLO Assessment Results

Each instructional and cocurricular program has a program assessment plan that defines the timing for the program's SLO assessment. As a result, assessment activities take place throughout the year. Additionally, recommended actions to improve programs are identified throughout the year. Annual program review is a time to collect and consider the results of and recommendations from the past year's SLO assessment activities.

Annual Program Review

During annual program review, each program's local leadership and practitioners review SLO assessment records and recommendations for improvements. These records are considered alongside any other assessment activities that might have occurred throughout the year, and a holistic set of recommendations for improvement is identified in a program improvement plan like the one shown in Figure 7.8. At the same time, institutional program leaders for instructional and cocurricular programs consider all improvements identified throughout the year that are institutional in nature and develop a final holistic set of institutional-level program improvements in a similarly structured plan.

The local and institutional program improvement plans are reviewed through established program review procedures. During this period of discussion and collaboration, conflicts or redundancies in local and institutional improvements are resolved, and local and institutional program improvement plans are finalized and included in local and institutional budgeting procedures. During the budgeting process, local and institutional leadership consider the recommended improvements within the context of other local and institutional priorities. The program improvement plan is then used to track whether a specific

Figure 7.8 Example of a program improvement plan.

Program Improvement Plan, 2008–2011

Program: Business Administration

Campus: Rancho Cordova

#	Date Added	Program	Area of Emphasis (Instructional Programs Only)	Action (Tactic)	Owner	Estimated Cost	Level of Change (1–2)	Target Completion Date	Revised Completion Date	Date Completed	For Change Level 2 ONLY			
											Approved	*Approved w/ Changes	*Not Approved	*Deferred
1	8/29/2008	Bus Admin	General	Implement "Wall of Fame" board for students that excel in OS101	DAA	None	1	Jan-09	Jul-10		X			X
2	8/29/2008	Bus Admin	General	Convene faculty advisory board on selection criteria	Program Director	None	1	Oct-08	Jul-10		X			X
3	8/29/2008	Bus Admin	General	Enable LRC logon tracking program	IT	None	1	Oct-08					X	
4	8/29/2008	Bus Admin	General	Create electronic folders to track students requesting tutoring	LRC Manager	None	1	Jan-09	Dec-09	Dec-09	X			X
5	8/29/2008	Bus Admin	General	Organize data collection for tutoring requests by subject	LRC Manager	None	1	Jan-09	Dec-09	Dec-09	X			X

improvement was approved, approved with changes, not approved, or deferred. Though not all program improvements are approved, institutional leadership makes a sincere effort to implement proposed recommendations that are both feasible and aligned with institutional priorities and goals. Heald ensures continued transparency by publishing program improvement plans and, after the budgeting period is finished, the approval status of each improvement.

Comprehensive Program Review

Comprehensive program review is scheduled to occur on multiyear cycles (currently five years) and follows procedures similar to those described for annual program review. Comprehensive program review is an opportunity to reflect on longitudinal data, improvements in student learning, and institutional SLO data. We also consider major revisions to instructional programs. The diagram in Figure 7.9 depicts how program review and the development

Figure 7.9 Heald College's planning process.

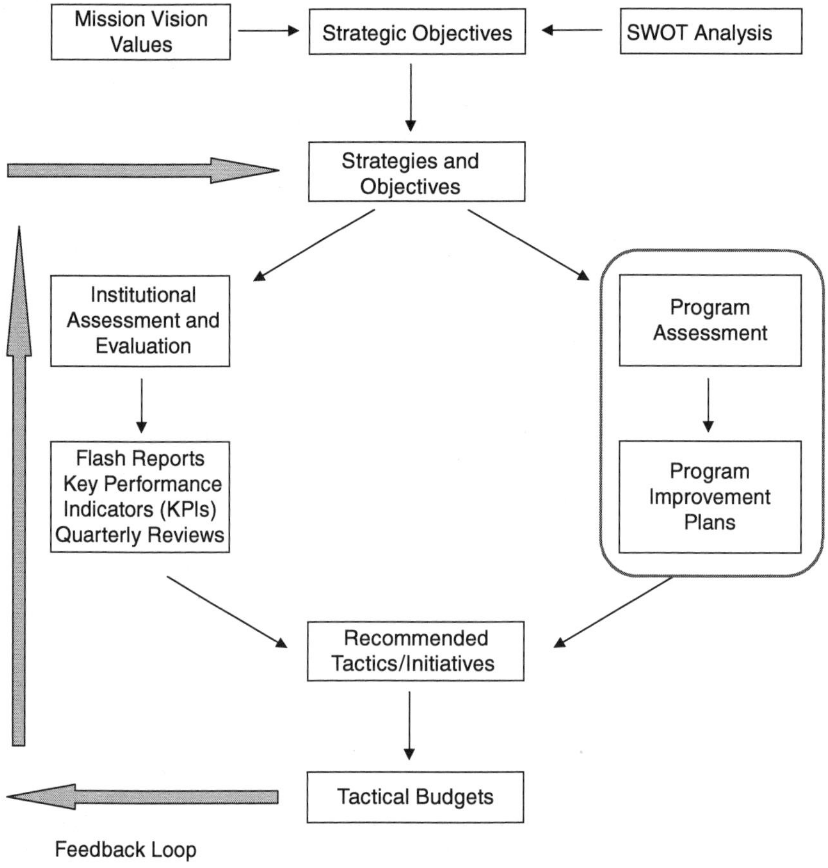

of program improvement plans fit within Heald's overall strategic planning and budgeting process.

Approved improvements identified through annual and comprehensive program review are implemented according to the program improvement plan. Local and institutional leaders are responsible for managing and tracking the completion of program improvement actions on time and within budget. Again, in an effort to communicate throughout the organization transparently, updates on the status of planned improvements are published and available to faculty and staff.

Summary of Heald's Experience

Heald's methods for using and communicating the results of SLO assessment have evolved significantly since systematic program review and SLO assessment was developed in 2008. The college has benefited from a spirit of self-reflection on assessment processes and has consistently improved the process each year. The improvements we have made have been primarily to create more scalable and streamlined processes, as well as enhance institutional effectiveness training at the local and institutional level. However, the basic tenets established early on—transparency, safety, and inclusiveness—continue to guide how the college uses and communicates the results of SLO assessment. Heald's success in this area can be attributed to a fundamental and persistent commitment to these tenets, and to the continued commitment and overt support of the president and CEO.

Conclusion

Heald College utilizes a number of strategies to create and support effective communication practices during the assessment process. Faculty and staff throughout the institution intentionally work together, utilizing a variety of agreed-upon tools and methods to "close the loop," using the results of assessment efforts to inform accountability measures and improve overall student learning and success.

In terms of communication, the implementation of assessment at Heald College supports the push for transparency and open dialogue throughout the entire process. As such, various "checks and balances" and tools for communication throughout all levels of the organization were created in an effort to ensure that the organizational culture promotes candid discussion, a shared knowledge base, and limited questions of intent or purpose. Moreover, the standardized communication channels allow for the collection of data in a timely and organized fashion. This communication supports the effective use of results and provides stakeholders with access to relevant and useful results that may be used to improve student learning and development.

Finally, Heald College's story illustrates the notion that good assessment practices, particularly those involving communication and the use of results, do not "happen overnight." Rather, the creation of a dynamic and useful assessment process that can be sustained over time requires a strong foundation of human, capital, and knowledge resources. Examples of those resources are provided in this chapter but may vary from institution to institution. The aforementioned foundation takes time to build and must be supported at all levels of the organization and by a majority of stakeholders within the organization. Once that foundation is built, however, effective communication and the use of results will stand out as hallmarks within the institutional culture, and improvement and accountability measures will be recognized by both internal and external constituents as valid and important to overall organizational and student success.

References

Bresciani, M. J., Moore Gardner, M., & Hickmott, J. (2009). *Demonstrating student success: A practical guide to outcomes-based assessment of learning and development in student affairs.* Sterling, VA: Stylus.

Maki, P. L. (2004). *Assessing for learning: Building a sustainable commitment across the institution.* Sterling, VA: Stylus.

Nichols, J. O., & Nichols, K. W. (2005). *A road map for improvement of student learning and support services through assessment.* New York, NY: Agathon Press.

Schuh, J., & Associates. (2008). *Assessment methods for student affairs.* San Francisco, CA: Jossey-Bass.

Suskie, L. (2009). *Assessing student learning: A common sense guide.* San Francisco, CA: Jossey-Bass.

8

DECISION MAKING IN THE LEARNING OUTCOMES ASSESSMENT PROCESS

Sandra Coyner and Sunday O. Faseyitan

I n this chapter we examine decision-making contexts, highlight decision-making issues in the process of implementing learning outcomes assessment in the community and two-year college environment, and describe how such issues were handled at a sample community college. The decision-making issues reflect the point of view of the administrators who manage the process, the faculty who facilitate the classroom teaching, and the student affairs/services professionals who are responsible for learning in the cocurriculum. The different roles that each group plays in the assessment process may contribute to prospective decision-making issues that often result in conflict. Utilizing decision-making models can assist the community and two-year college professional in effectively navigating the process, and, depending on specific issues and the dominant organizational structure utilized by the institution (e.g., bureaucratic, collegial, political, anarchical, or cybernetic), such models may help reduce conflict and strengthen the overall institutional assessment experience.

We concentrate on decisions that impact the process of learning outcomes assessment and discuss the subsequent changes that are necessary in curriculum, instruction, and student support services to improve student learning. Moreover, we contend that effective assessment, which may be used to enhance student learning, demonstrate accountability, and improve overall programs and services, is contingent upon sound decision making to ensure the realization of a sustainable process.

After reading this chapter, the reader will be able to recognize decision-making contexts in the assessment process, describe five decision-making considerations that could affect the success of the student learning outcome (SLO) process from three important stakeholder perspectives, and utilize decision-making models to analyze decision considerations in the SLO assessment process through a community college case study.

Roles and Responsibilities for SLO Assessment

There are three important stakeholders in the learning outcome assessment process: (a) administrators, in this case comprising vice presidents in charge of academic affairs or student affairs, deans of academic divisions and student services, and deans and directors of assessment; (b) the teaching faculty; and (c) student affairs/services professionals.

Administrators consider student learning an important way to demonstrate achievement of the college's mission and therefore have attempted to develop a culture in their colleges that favors using assessment to measure institutional effectiveness and instructional achievement and determine areas that need improvement. Administrators tend to make top-down decisions to institute some type of campus assessment initiative (Ewell, 2008). The structure of the learning outcomes assessment process depends on the predominant type of organizational functioning, institutional size, culture, and in particular whether there is the presence of a labor union. The role of the administrator is to facilitate the process and act as a change agent to move the college toward becoming a learning organization.

In the community and two-year college environment, student learning occurs in both the academic and cocurricular environment. Classroom experiences are characterized by well-structured syllabi that teach students general education skills such as written and oral communication, math and computational skills, information literacy, critical thinking, and wellness; and major-programs-of-study skills such as business management, chemistry, math, engineering, education, psychology, and nursing. Teaching faculty bear responsibility for the syllabi, delivery of instruction, and assessment of student performance in the course, which culminates in the award of an earned grade at the end of the semester. With the new emphasis on student learning, faculty who develop syllabi are expected to develop the learning outcomes for associate's degree programs, appropriate measures and standards for student achievement of the intended learning outcome. Not all faculty, however, have embraced this responsibility cheerfully, citing many reasons for resistance, including inadequate time, limited resources, lack of top-down support, and infringement upon academic freedom.

Student affairs/services professionals provide cocurricular learning opportunities to support and enhance learning in the classroom and to foster physical and emotional well-being and social development. This integration of student services and academics in a holistic process is important to support student learning and development (American College Personnel Association et al., 2006). At community and two-year colleges, students are expected to leave the college with skills in setting and executing goals, transitioning from college to work, transferring requirements for baccalaureate studies, and so forth. As noted in preceding chapters, measurable student learning objectives and outcomes can be developed for the cocurricular environment in the same manner as is commonly done for the general education program and major programs of study. Moreover, when cocurricular learning outcomes are intentionally coupled with similar outcomes in the academic classroom, student learning and development will be deeper and more meaningful (Bresciani, Moore Gardner, & Hickmott, 2009).

Models for Analyzing Decision Making in Higher Education

Decision making in higher education is multifaceted. It requires a choice among a set of alternatives and consideration of possible consequences to solve a problem. Rationalism, implying that there should be a reasonable connection between the means and the end based on information or knowledge, is presumed. However, Hoy and Tarter (2008) believe that "non-rational choice is the natural state" (p. 3). They note that decision making is driven by normative and affective considerations. Etzioni (1989) eschews rationalism as "a deeply optimistic approach that assumes we can learn all we need to know" (p. 124). Models can be useful and help guide decision making to achieve a desired outcome in different situations with different decision goals.

Before considering the decision-making process best suited to a situation, it is essential to consider higher education institutional characteristics and personality within which the decision will occur. Birnbaum (1988) describes the structure of academic organizations and the challenges of decision making within higher education institutions. He identifies four models of organizational functioning and suggests a fifth institutional prototype, identifying the important characteristics of each as they provide context for the decision-making environment in higher education. The models of organizational functioning are collegial, bureaucratic, political, anarchical, and cybernetic.

Collegial institutions emphasize shared power and favor consensus for decision making. Faculty and academic administrators are fairly homogeneous in their academic preparation, degree attainment, and they share a sense of community and institutional culture. Administrators are often faculty members who "agree to serve for a limited time and then return to their classroom responsibilities" (Birnbaum, 1988, p. 89). There is a distinct respect for the collegial process because administrators and faculty view themselves collectively. Collegial institutions tend to be comparatively small and value relationships. Decision making through a collegial process can be cumbersome; however, it also offers an in-depth exploration of alternatives and possibilities. Deliberations during the decision-making process provide opportunities for solutions that are well vetted.

Hierarchy, organizational charts, and vertical authority, as described by Birnbaum (1988), characterize *bureaucratic institutions*. Structure is emphasized, as are rules, regulations, and other formal processes established by rational processes. This model of organizational functioning boasts efficiency and effectiveness. Although decision making would appear to benefit from this structure regarding routine decisions, nonroutine decisions that are complex and challenging may be more problematic.

Political institutions utilize obtained power to influence decisions to benefit a particular group or groups. Especially in times of scarce resources, these groups and subgroups attempt to use power to influence policies. Although it might appear that this maneuvering could have seriously detrimental effects on the institution, Birnbaum (1988) notes,

> Individuals belong to more than one group, and they participate in many political processes, each of which involves different people. The existence of a large number of small cross-cutting disagreements provides checks and balances against major disruptions, so that the agitation of political processes can ironically lead to system stability. (p. 136)

The *anarchical* model of organizational functioning offers a description of the institution as a "community of autonomous actors" (Birnbaum, 1988, p. 151). Three distinct characteristics of an anarchical institution are problematic goals, unclear technology, and fluid participation (Birnbaum, 1988). Problematic goals may include ambiguity, competition, and/or changing philosophies. *Technology*, as defined by Birnbaum (1988), is "the characteristic processes through which organizations convert inputs to outputs" (p. 155). Fluid participation describes the dynamic nature of administrative and faculty participation in organizational activities. Participation levels can change based on interest, assignments, opportunities, and attention. Because individuals are involved in the decision-making process, it can be unpredictable in this environment. Further, fluidity contributes to confusion, and ambiguity and uncertainty invade the decision-making process.

Birnbaum (1988) advocates a *cybernetic* approach for higher education institutions integrating elements of the previous models to allow decision making through self-regulation and effective administration. Cybernetic controls respond to inputs and utilize feedback to detect and correct problems. This enables an institution to be responsive and make decisions as needed within an ever-changing educational and administrative environment. When the institution is viewed as a system comprising numerous subsystems functioning as miniature systems within the whole, decision making in this setting is independent, dependent, and dynamic. Recognizing that leaders may not fully understand or be aware of all the institution's activities and issues within each system and subsystem, Birnbaum (1988) notes that doing nothing may be a better decision than doing something involving situations with unknowns.

Once the institutional context is identified, the decision-making process can commence. However, there are two important pre-decision steps in the decision-making process. The first step, regardless of the decision-making model best suited for the task, is to ask, "Do I make this decision?" Absent of decision-making responsibility, do not proceed any further. The second pre-decision step requires an examination of the impending decision to determine whether it is routine (programmed) or nonroutine (nonprogrammed). Routine decisions involve problems with alternatives specified in advance. There are typically procedures that already exist to handle the problem. Nonroutine decisions involve more complex, uncommon, or infrequent problems with no alternative specified in advance. These nonroutine decisions require a thoughtful approach.

Upon determining the actual need for decision making and consideration regarding the type of organizational functioning present in the higher education institution, models can be helpful to provide perspectives on the process and possible advantages and disadvantages offered by different methods. Based on the myriad factors involved in many decisions and on the variance among institutions, colleges, departments, and programs, no one model will fit all situations. Familiarity with alternative decision-making processes enables decision makers at community and two-year institutions the flexibility to select the best options for their specific assessment process.

Classical Decision-Making Model

The classical decision-making model is predicated on the notion that all decisions should be rational. It favors a linear progression of steps: identifying the problem, identifying potential causes and diagnosing the problem, identifying alternatives to solve the problem, considering consequences, evaluating alternatives, selecting the best alternative, implementing the decision, and evaluating the results (Hoy & Tarter, 2008). This model assumes an optimizing strategy and that there are clear goals, availability of complete information, and the capacity to understand the problem fully. Based on the number of variables present in any situation, the need for absolutes in order to make decisions is problematic. Also called the rational decision-making model, this model requires too many variables, many of which may be either unknown or unavailable. Etzioni (1967) notes that "a decision-maker, attempting to adhere to the tenets of a rationalistic model, will become frustrated, exhaust his resources without coming to a decision, and remain without an effective decision-making model to guide him" (p. 386). In addition, Hoy and Miskel (2001) note that this model is not very useful for most decisions.

Administrative Model

In contrast to the rational rigidity of the classical model, Simon (1997) recognizes the need for good decisions in order to provide a satisfactory organizational outcome. Satisficing enables acceptable decisions to be reached without the constraint of finding the "perfect" solution. This practical approach acknowledges that solving one problem may lead to other problems and that the classical model fails to provide flexibility to enable decision makers to arrive at a decision that although not optimal meets the objectives of problem solving. Simon (1997) considers the influences of values and facts on administrative decision making. This straightforward model supports identifying the considerations for a decision and then selecting the first solution to meet those considerations to produce a satisfactory outcome.

Incremental Model

"Muddling through" characterizes Lindblom's (1959) incremental decision-making model. The objectives and alternatives required by the classical model are often rigid, and because satisficing can be challenging due to changing aspects of the decision and its components, incrementalism features gradual and progressive considerations to best reflect the changing decision-making landscape and elements for consideration. By muddling through the process and making small decisions along the way, there can be more agreement by participants and the overwhelming complexity of a large decision is reduced into more manageable fragments. Intertwining objectives and alternatives enables decision makers to accurately assess decisions made along the way through continual comparisons.

Mixed-Scanning Model

Etzioni (1967, 1986, 1989) viewed the decision-making process as inclusive of rational and incremental satisficing decisions and developed a mixed-scanning approach. Mixed scanning maintains the need for adaptive satisficing with the goal of making a decision that satisfices by removing the least desirable solutions and selecting from the options that remain. Incremental decisions are made to accept or reject information, and the resulting decision is a product of sorting through alternatives and information during the decision-making process. Guidelines for using a mixed-scanning strategy include using focused trial and error, proceeding slowly, procrastinating, staggering decisions, fractionalizing and testing subdecisions, hedging bets by implementing several alternatives and adjusting, and employing reversible decisions (Etzioni, 1989). This ongoing analysis and adaptation enables some action to be taken while systematically assessing and modifying incremental decisions aimed at a satisfactory final outcome.

Garbage Can Model

Considering institutions as organized anarchies characterized by problematic preferences, unclear technology, and fluid participation, Cohen, March, and Olsen (1972) advocate a garbage can model of decision making. They contend that the chaotic nature of an organization lends itself to a decision-making process that is more reflective of the independent nature of the problems, personnel, alternatives, and solutions involved than other models allow. In this model, items are "dumped" into the garbage can, where they may lose their identity, connectedness, and relationship but are available for use when needed. The hope is that the garbage can will serve as a repository containing alternatives and solutions that will be useful as problems arise over time. Although this model does recognize the systematic interrelatedness present in higher education institutions, Cohen et al. note:

> It is clear that the garbage can process does not resolve problems well. But it does enable choices to be made and problems resolved, even when the organization is plagued with goal ambiguity and conflict, with poorly understood problems that wander in and out of the system, with a variable environment, and with decision makers who may have other things on their minds. (p. 16)

Decision-Making Issues in the SLO Assessment Process

Five issues for which decision making is critical to the SLO process are the intended learning outcomes, measurement tools and data collection and analysis, design of the assessment process, postassessment activities, and methods for promoting a culture of evidence. These decision issues are consistent with those areas that are common to assessment challenges in both two- and four-year institutions as identified by Nunley, Bers, and Manning (2011). They identified four broad areas (determining what to measure, ensuring real institutional commitment, effectively engaging faculty, and selecting valid and reliable instruments) and 11 challenges that community colleges face when involved in learning outcomes assessment. The following sections address important decisions concerning community college assessments.

Issue 1: Decisions Regarding Intended Learning Outcomes

Although the decision on what the intended learning outcomes will be depends on the institution, the expectations of accrediting bodies and the relevant professional organizations, as well as the economic and social needs of the community, often have significant considerations. For example, the Middle States Commission on Higher Education recommends six program competencies for general education (Middle States Commission on Higher Education, Characteristics of Excellence in Higher Education, p. 47), and nearly all institutions have the accrediting body's suggestion as a minimum for their member institutions. Program-level intended outcomes are mostly derived from the collective expertise of the faculty and student affairs/services professionals and are often influenced by local needs articulated by business and industry and sometimes by accrediting agencies in the discipline. These accrediting agencies may include the Accreditation Board for Engineering and Technology, the National League for Nursing Accrediting Commission, and the Accreditation Council for Business Schools and Programs.

Another consideration for decisions in community and two-year colleges is transferability. In crafting a program that represents the first two years of a four-year baccalaureate program, the program's intended outcome is seamless transfer so that the student transfers as a junior. Faculty creating the program must be familiar with changes in the curriculum of the four-year colleges to which their students generally transfer. Student affairs/services professions, such as transfer counselors in community and two-year colleges, have to be familiar with articulation agreements and possible changes in general education requirements in four-year institutions in order to advise students on the correct courses to take to adequately prepare them for the school to which they wish to transfer.

Many institutions are just warming up to SLOs for student affairs/services, and there are suggestions for intended learning outcomes for such departments. Schuh and Gansemer-Topf (2010) note that student affairs professionals could assess learning that results from participating in a club or an organization, a leadership development program, fraternities or sororities, or living in a residence hall. As noted earlier, by intentionally coupling cocurricular and academic learning outcomes, community and two-year institutions can strengthen the impact of students' education experiences and contribute to much deeper holistic student learning and development. Decision making during the assessment process should continually focus on ways to share resources and collaborate between curricular and cocurricular programs and services.

Additionally, the intended learning outcomes for programs and student services must be tied to the community college mission and vision. This is best

TABLE 8.1
Decision areas for stakeholders regarding intended learning outcomes.

Administrator	Oversee general education and program learning outcomes to ensure they align with accreditation requirements and business and industry needs.
	Develop tactics to encourage faculty members and student affairs professionals to create learning goals and outcomes for courses and services and link them to program outcomes.
	Provide support for faculty and staff development on effective assessment of student learning.
Faculty	Develop measurable learning outcomes for general education and program majors.
	Write the outcome statements, the means of assessment, and the standard for success.
	Align the curriculum with outcomes statements using curriculum mapping.
Student Affairs Professional	Develop measurable learning outcomes for cocurricular programs and services.
	Write the outcome statements, the means of assessment, and the standard for success.

accomplished through a collaborative decision-making process in which stakeholders share their visions of what students are expected to learn as they experience the college programs. Table 8.1 provides decision areas for stakeholders.

Issue 2: Decisions Regarding Measurement Tools, Data Collection, and Data Analysis

After a well-thought-out list of intended learning outcomes has been developed for general education, major areas of study, and student services, faculty and student services professionals must determine measurement tools and articulate the expected student performances before embarking on data collection. Examples of typical measurement tools include tests, portfolios, projects, surveys, interviews, and focus groups. It is important to use instruments that are valid and reliable. To have robust analysis, multiple instruments should be used to collect data from multiple sources and the results should be triangulated. SLO data could come from students, faculty, employers, transfer institutions, and other institutional stakeholders. Every effort should be made to include direct and indirect measures. Direct measures should reflect information that faculty members and student affairs/services professionals can use to improve student learning. Moreover, when an "outside"

TABLE 8.2

Decision areas for stakeholders regarding measurement tools, data collection, and data analysis.

Administrator	Determine the frequency of data collection (e.g., every three years).
	Create a collaborative process with faculty members and student affairs/services professionals on the design of the assessment method to ensure validity and reliability and to identify samples and sampling methods.
	Identify how best to document data for analysis.
	Select the method of reporting data.
Faculty	Design assessment methods that collect valid and reliable data for the purpose of improving student learning.
	Integrate the evaluation of higher order thinking (Blooms Taxonomy).
	Determine the quantity of data necessary to make decisions on how to improve student learning.
Student Affairs Professional	Design an assessment method that collects valid and reliable data on learning, personal development, and student development as a result of the college experience.
	Determine how to measure important attributes or behaviors that are expected to change, and compare the attributes and behaviors of participants and nonparticipants in the program.
	Determine the quantity of data necessary to make decisions on how to improve student learning, personal development, and student development.

instrument is to be used, it is necessary to engage the instructor or student affairs/services professional in the selection of the instrument to make sure that it aligns well with the intended outcomes. Otherwise, he or she may be less likely to use the results to improve academic and cocurricular programs and services (Banta & Pike, 2012; Suskie, 2009).

Decisions about frequency of data collection, administrative support, management of the process, analysis, and reporting of data are important and should be made at the onset of the development of a comprehensive assessment plan. Table 8.2 provides decision areas for stakeholders.

Issue 3: Decisions Regarding the Process

The assessment of SLOs is necessary to earn accreditation and accreditors require that a college or university describe the process. The Middle States Commission

TABLE 8.3
Decision areas for stakeholders regarding the process.

Administrator	Organize the process and articulate functions that are centralized and decentralized.
	Find ways to collaborate on activities during and after the assessment process (e.g., faculty and administrator conference on assessment results).
	Provide administrative, technical, and financial support.
	Support professional development opportunities and resources for faculty members and student affairs professionals to learn how to assess student learning and improve teaching and curricula.
Faculty	Provide leadership in the collection and review of data.
	Analyze classroom assessment practices and their outcomes.
	Participate in professional development opportunities.
	Collaborate and communicate throughout the process.
Student Affairs Professional	Provide leadership in the collection and review of data.
	Analyze classroom assessment practices and their outcomes.
	Participate in professional development opportunities.
	Collaborate and communicate throughout the process.

on Higher Education (2011), for example, asks for "a documented, organized and sustained assessment process to evaluate and improve student learning" (p. 66). The expectation is that the process include support of faculty and administrators in assessing and responding to assessment results, show realistic guidelines and timetables, and use multiple measures. Furthermore, a good process must show that assessment information is shared and discussed with appropriate constituents and is used as part of institutional assessment.

Additionally, it is important to implement a consistent process across the institution in order to reduce ambiguity, increase transparency, standardize documentation, and make it easier for evaluators to examine documentation. Table 8.3 provides decision areas for stakeholders.

Issue 4: Decisions Regarding Postassessment—"Closing the Loop"

Postassessment decisions are based on steps that will lead to improvement. This is often referred to as "closing the loop." Reviewing assessment results in relation to the course work and program goals is an important part of

TABLE 8.4
Decision areas for stakeholders regarding postassessment.

Administrator	Report and share the assessment information.
	Encourage campuswide efforts to assess student learning and improve learning and development.
	Develop and communicate a shared calendar for closing-the-loop activities.
Faculty	Review assessment methods.
	Determine how to improve courses and student learning of course objectives.
	Develop and participate in authentic dialogue with colleagues on student learning and improvement strategies.
	Implement strategies.
	Collect new data after implementation.
Student Affairs Professional	Review assessment methods.
	Determine ways to improve programs and services.
	Develop and participate in authentic dialogue with colleagues on student learning and improvement strategies.
	Implement assessment strategies.
	Collect new data after implementation.

the assessment process. Discussions should focus on topics including student learning, effective teaching, the curriculum, course sequencing, and program development and delivery. The purpose here is to critically examine the results and determine what actions should be taken to influence learning through small and direct instructional or student support actions. All the stakeholders should be involved, and actions to be taken when the target is met or not met should be identified and communicated. For example, such actions might vary from just concluding that learning performance meets expectations to making a major curriculum or programmatic change, or conducting remediation, adding prerequisites, or changing assignments.

Closing the loop is a challenge in the assessment process, as demonstrated by a study by Banta and Blaich (2010) in which they found that too few faculty members are studying assessment findings to see what improvements might be suggested and making and taking appropriate steps to implement them. Table 8.4 provides decision areas for stakeholders.

Issue 5: Decisions Regarding Promoting a Culture of Evidence

For assessment to be successful, all stakeholders must demonstrate and promote the use of data for decision making. Increased institutional buy-in

TABLE 8.5
Decision areas for stakeholders regarding promoting a culture of evidence.

Administrator	Build a process that allows for trust, pedagogy, and sound reflections.
	Demonstrate that decision making on campus is based on analytics.
	Articulate the benefits of the assessment process.
	Support professional development workshops.
Faculty	Engage in authentic discussions/reflections with peers on assessment results.
	Focus on how well your students are learning.
	Commit to improving instructional effectiveness and the curriculum.
Student Affairs Professional	Engage in authentic discussions/reflections with peers on assessment results.
	Focus on how well cocurricular experiences enhance and promote student learning and development.
	Commit to improving program effectiveness and student development.

as a whole results from the transparent and easily identifiable use of assessment results for improvement and change. Actively utilizing assessment results to inform major institutional decisions, such as budgeting, strategic planning, or curriculum development, will result in an increased understanding of the value of such information and a stronger desire by stakeholders to participate in the process (Bresciani et al., 2009). Moreover, faculty members' approval of the assessment process at an institution has been found to be connected to factors such as believable results that can be acted upon, an emphasis on the use of assessment for academic improvement, surety that the assessment efforts have desirable payoff for students and faculty, and an awareness of how external factors such as accreditation influence their work (Grunwald & Peterson, 2003). Table 8.5 provides decision areas for stakeholders.

Case Study: Decision Making at Butler County Community College

In 1999, Butler County Community College adopted the Nichols five-column model for assessing the effectiveness of the administrative and academic support units. Directors, deans, and vice presidents attended a workshop led by the director of institutional research that demonstrated the use of the model for program effectiveness. The model is similar to the performance and appraisal system that all administrators already use, so it was not a hard sell. In 2002, the deans were then charged with adopting the model for the assessment of student learning at the associate degree program level. The academic unit has four divisions: Humanities and Social Sciences, Business, Science and Technology, and Nursing and Allied Health. Each dean attempted to lead faculty in his or her division to develop program learning outcomes, measures of achievement for the graduates, and standards for success. Faculty reactions varied, mostly by discipline groups. Liberal arts disciplines did not believe that learning can be measured the way you can measure skills in science and technology, business, and nursing. Programs that have discipline accreditations could relate to the assessment of student learning, but it had not taken hold in their discipline accreditation standards. Natural science faculty could not see how this process would positively affect teaching and learning. In general, faculty resistance was typical. Each division decided on the structure, including who would develop the learning outcome and the measures, who would collect data and how often the data would be collected, who would analyze the data and how the data would be reported.

By the start of the accreditation self-study process in 2005, the four divisions had different levels of success. Instructors considered the assessment of SLOs another bureaucratic government agenda that would go away if resisted long enough. Many who did the assessment just wanted to get it over with, and they figured that after accreditation visitors were gone, they would relax for five to 10 years.

The college administration found that underneath these faculty postures is the lack of confidence in this type of assessment. Higher education instructors are experts in their disciplines, not in assessment. To reduce their fears it was decided that ongoing faculty development would be part of the strategy to accomplish an appreciation for assessment and the use of evidence to improve instructions.

The vice president for academic affairs devoted a professional day to discuss with faculty the importance of the assessment of associate degree programs for accreditation purposes but more so for the improvement of teaching and learning. The vice president and the coordinator of academic assessment also visited each of the four divisions to reinforce the importance of carrying out the tasks of assessment. The deans provided assistance in writing program competencies, determining measures for success, and creating targets and benchmarks.

The next roadblock to assessment in the journey was data collection. Faculty wanted to use the same grading that they used in their classes. When they realized that specific program competencies were being measured and the data needed would be different from their normal end-of-semester grade tally, they repelled doing the task. Some referred to this task as over and above their normal duty and stated they needed additional compensation. It has become an issue that the faculty union puts on labor negotiation. To make the data collection process uniform across campus, the assessment unit developed a template for data collection and analysis.

In order to focus the college's assessment efforts, an assessment office was created in 2008 to design an assessment process, delineate the decision issues for all stakeholders, and foster the cultivation of a culture of evidence among faculty and staff. At the time of this writing, the college achieved success in defining the program's intended learning outcomes for all 60 associate degree programs and limited success in data collection. The assessment process is in place and appears to be robust. Closing the loop has been achieved on 5% of the competencies that were assessed. Implementing this SLO process has resulted in faculty and staff cultivating a culture of evidence on campus and putting in place performance-based strategic planning and resource allocation.

Conclusion

Establishing an SLO assessment process in a community or two-year college is a challenge because such institutions often struggle with limited human and capital resources. Effective decision making within the assessment process is therefore essential to building a self-sustaining system. In an effort to assist higher education professionals at community and two-year colleges with the creation of such an effective and sustainable assessment process, we have detailed a key part of the assessment process, decision making. More specifically, we have presented an overview of decision-making models, identified five areas where decision making is critical to the process—determining the intended learning outcomes, measurement tools and data collection, the design of the assessment process, postassessment activities, and methods for promoting a culture of evidence—and provided a case study to illustrate the need for effective decision making.

Assessment of student learning is still new to the higher education culture, and, depending on the decision goals, stakeholders will have to determine whether they need to be collegial, bureaucratic, or political in strategy. Problem-solving techniques using administrative, incremental, mixed-scanning, or garbage can models of decision making may be used to inform the decision-making process. However, given the loosely coupled higher education organization, a collaborative decision-making model may be best for an SLO assessment process. Regardless of the decision-making models utilized, it is important that all stakeholders work hand in hand to have a shared understanding of the reasons behind the process, the assessment process itself, and the ways in which the results will be used for improvement and accountability. The stakeholders will likely be responsible for different aspects of the decision areas, and these decisions must complement each other for learning and assessment to be whole and successful. Each stakeholder must understand others' perspectives, and the information relevant to decision making is best obtained when everyone is at the table.

As noted throughout the chapter, the design of the assessment process should foster collaboration. Decisions about evaluating the results and sharing the results should be made collaboratively among stakeholders. To promote a culture of evidence all stakeholders must demonstrate decision making based on analytics and focus on improving student learning and development based on assessment results.

The assessment of student learning will continue in higher education for the foreseeable future, and developing an effective process will make the change less stressful for faculty and staff alike. The success and sustainability of the process depend on the point of view and the collaboration of all the stakeholders.

References

American College Personnel Association, Association of College and University Housing Officers–International, Association of College Unions–International, National Academic Advising Association, National Association for Campus Activities, National Association of Student Personnel Administrators, & National Intramural-Recreational Sports Association. (2006). *Learning reconsidered 2: A practical guide to implementing a campus-wide focus on the student experience.* Retrieved from www.myacpa.org/pub/documents/LearningReconsidered2.pdf

Banta, T. W., & Blaich, C. (2010). Closing the assessment loop. *Change Magazine, 43*(1), 22–27. doi:10.1080/00091383.2011.538642

Banta, T. W., & Pike, G. R. (2012). The bottom line: Will faculty use assessment findings? In C. Secolsky & B. Denison (Eds.), *Handbook on measurement, assessment, and evaluation in higher education* (pp. 47–56). New York, NY: Routledge.

Birnbaum, R. (1988). *How colleges work: The cybernetics of academic organization and leadership.* San Francisco, CA: Jossey-Bass.

Bresciani, M. J., Moore Gardner, M., & Hickmott, J. (2009). *Demonstrating student success: A practical guide to outcomes-based assessment of learning and development in student affairs.* Sterling, VA: Stylus.

Cohen, M. D., March, J. G., & Olsen, J. P. (1972). A garbage can model of organizational choice. *Administrative Science Quarterly, 17*(1), 1–25. Retrieved from http://links.jstor.org/sici?sici=0001-8392%28197203%2917%3A1%3C1%3AA GCMOO%3E2.0CO%3B2-9

Etzioni, A. (1967). Mixed-scanning: A "third" approach to decision-making. *Public Administration Review, 27*(5), 385–392. Retrieved from http://links.jstor.org/sici?sici=0033-3352%281967l2%2927%3A5%3C385%3AMA%22ATD%3E2.0.CO%3B2-N

Etzioini, A. (1986). Mixed scanning revised. *Public Administration Review, 46*, 8–15.

Etzioni, A. (1989). Humble decision making. *Harvard Business Review, 67*, 122–126.

Ewell, P. T. (2008). *U.S. accreditation and the future of quality assurance: A tenth anniversary report from the Council on Higher Education Accreditation.* Washington, DC: CHEA Institute for Research and Study of Accreditation and Quality Assurance.

Grunwald, H., & Peterson, M. W. (2003). Factors that promote faculty involvement in and satisfaction with institutional and classroom student assessment. *Research in Higher Education, 44*(2), 173–204.

Hoy, W., & Miskel, C. (2001). *Educational administration: Theory, research, and practice* (6th ed.). New York, NY: McGraw-Hill.

Hoy, W. K., & Tarter, C. J. (2008). *Administrators solving the problems of practice: Decision-making cases, concepts, and consequences* (3rd ed.). Boston, MA: Pearson.

Lindblom, C. E. (1959). The science of "muddling through." *Public Administration Review, 19*(2), 79–88. Retrieved from http://links.jstor.org/sici?sici=0033-3352%281959l2%2919%3A2%3C79%3ATSO%22T%3E2.0.CO%3B2-7

Middle States Commission on Higher Education. (2011). *Characteristics of excellence in Higher Education.* Retrieved from www.msche.org/publications/CHX06060320124919.pdf

Nunley, C., Bers, T., & Manning, T. (2011, July). *Learning outcomes assessment in community colleges* (NILOA Occasional Paper No. 10). Urbana, IL: University of Illinois, National Institute for Learning Outcomes Assessment. Retrieved from http://www.learningoutcomeassessment.org/occasionalpaperten.htm

Schuh, J. H., & Gansemer-Topf, A. M. (2010). *The role of student affairs in student learning assessment* (NILOA Occasional Paper No. 7). Urbana, IL: University of Illinois, National Institute for Learning Outcomes Assessment. Retrieved from http://www.learningoutcomeassessment.org/occasionalpaperseven.htm

Simon, H. A. (1997). *Administrative behavior: A study of decision-making processes in administrative organizations* (4th ed.). New York, NY: Free Press.

Suskie, L. (2009). *Assessing student learning: A common sense guide* (2nd ed.). San Francisco, CA: Jossey-Bass.

9

INCORPORATING OUTCOMES-BASED ASSESSMENT INTO PROGRAM REVIEW AND BUDGETING

David P. Eppich and Marilee J. Bresciani

It is no secret that we are operating within an environment that is continually experiencing change. Some of this change has always been attributable
to changes in demographics in students, technologies, and our understanding about what is the most effective and efficient way to prepare students.
However, the global economic crisis, concern about the value of a degree,
whether a two- or four-year degree, and concern about exactly what we are preparing students for in the future when we seemingly cannot even manage the
crisis of the present all seem to complicate this environment of change. All of
these pressing issues appear to be aggravating the tax-paying public's need for
accountability, which leads to conversations about performance-based funding models. These models themselves vary across states, and these variances
include changes in actual measurement points of indicators as well as acceptable standards of performance.

Strategic planning—which encompasses the need to manage resources
at the macro level—is strongly tied to the concept of outcomes-based assessment program review (Bresciani, Moore Gardner, & Hickmott, 2009; Freeman, Bresciani, & Bresciani, 2004). As institutional goals and outcomes are
prepared, the learning experience must align with the overall plan of the institution and be informed by measurement and evaluation to ensure its validity,
relevance, and continued innovation. The need to promote an organizational

culture that is responsive and even proactive of change is imperative if decades of traditional practice are to be redirected to meet the needs of students and promote an institution-wide environment of active learning.

A first step in the role of leadership is to ensure the education of organizational members as they relate to the positive aspects of change. This will in turn ensure a successful alignment and reallocation of resources to needed improvements (Crowley, 2011; Kouzes & Posner, 2008; Wheatley, 2006). The concept of organizational members and leaders being able to adapt to the changing environment denotes a concept of learning that must occur within the organization (van Eijnatten & Putnik, 2004; Wheatley, 2006). The education of organizational members further ensures a common basis for the adaptation that is so important in a group collaborating for change.

An Example of Managing Resource Planning

The student services departments at San Juan College began their change process by participating in a book review of *Leadership and the New Science* (Wheatley, 2006). Over the course of several months, chapter content was presented by departmental teams and discussed by participants. The book illustrated how organizations can learn to engage a continual state of change by welcoming the opening of new discovery and experimenting with different approaches (Wheatley, 2006). The engagement of ideas presented in the book not only created an environment that welcomed change but also launched organizational members on a learning journey in which they embraced their roles as both students and teachers. Following the shared book reading, the "realities" of the continually changing environment, which helped to catalyze this change, were explained to members of the organization. These "realities" were couched in a need to understand the changes in funding and measurements that had arisen in order to address the continually changing environment. Furthermore, the desire for students to engage in a holistic learning environment with all members of a campus community also played an integral role in organizational members' ability to understand the need for change. Both academic and student affairs/services leadership should be aware; however, that change can destabilize an organization and may be risky (Soparnot, 2011). It is important to ensure that the organizational change is consistent with the overall strategic plan and follows the mission, vision, and values of the institution.

A strategic plan for San Juan College was implemented in 2006 and the need for change was identified for student services prior to the reading of Wheatley's (2006) book. The college's new strategic plan was recently completed, undergoing revisions informed by a dynamic environmental scanning process, furthering the change paradigm for student services. The college now articulates its mission as follows: "to inspire and support life-long learning to achieve personal and community goals by providing quality education, services, and cultural enrichment" (San Juan College, 2013a). The vision statement is: "San Juan College will be an innovative, dynamic learning college built on mutual respect, meaningful participation and a collective commitment to students, the community and the core values of a comprehensive community college" (2013a).

Core values are reflected through the college's pledge of "I CARE," which stands for innovation, collaboration, accountability, respect, and excellence. Members of the college community believe that organizational values are critical for creating a learning environment in which faculty, staff, and students adhere to high standards and principles. They further believe that organizational leadership has the key role in embodying this belief because leaders must "model the behaviors they want to see in those who report to them" (Rhoades, 2011, p. 119).

San Juan College is committed to serving the needs of students and the community through a process of continuous quality improvement, incorporating the values of "I CARE." Some components of the values that provide support for the efforts of student services in the active learning of students are initiation of strategic change (innovation), collective wisdom (collaboration), assessment that leads to improvement (accountability), student-centered learning (respect), and modeling and developing of best practices (excellence).

The strategic goals of the college defined the initiatives, which are used by departments and staff members in those departments to further the mission of the college. For example, the goals for student services and the college state the following:

1. Establish well-defined policies, procedures and processes that advance the strategic plan.
2. Provide high quality student services that mitigate obstacles, promote learning and goal attainment.
3. Develop partnerships with industry, community, and other academic institutions that enhance student learning and the economic vitality of the region.
4. Develop systems for broad-based participation in data-informed decision making.
5. Allocate resources that promote institutional effectiveness.
6. Develop new resources and revenue streams to support operational and programmatic needs.

7. Provide resources and professional development for faculty and staff that support the Learning College philosophy within the comprehensive community college model.
8. Collaborate with regional leaders to drive economic development in the Four Corners.
9. Serve as a center for the arts, cultural enrichment and a resource for multi-cultural understanding.
10. Build widespread awareness of college programs, activities and services from which the College's stakeholders can benefit. (San Juan College, 2013b)

The desire and ability of all members of the departments to understand the mission, vision, and strategic initiatives for the entire college are important to provide a foundation for their work on a daily basis and to create the context for the learning atmosphere in which each member will engage students. Members of student services know the values expressed provide for the enriched culture of the college and create the environment in which employees can thrive (Rhoades, 2011). The engagement of values also created for students an appropriately modeled learning atmosphere, which often transcends verbalized behavior desires. Further steps that the student services departments enacted to achieve these espoused values are discussed in the next section.

Creating Linkages for Program Development and Strategic Planning

The strategic goals and mission of San Juan College are portrayed in the work of student services as efforts are made on an annual basis to engage in a thorough discussion with departmental directors on the mission of the student services area and the strategic initiatives that will be worked on in the upcoming year. The strategic goals set by the college and the student services area must be communicated to and embraced by departmental members in order to carry out those goals and maintain focus on the outcomes. The student services departments have created a flow pattern that attempts to work through the cycle of strategic goal attainment while incorporating the components of a comprehensive organization within the process. Figure 9.1 reflects this cycle.

Student services departments have each created their respective mission and vision that link back to the overall college while prescribing a mission that is theirs to carry out. The vision portrayed by each department also works to accomplish this linkage back to the vision of the college. The values describing the culture of the college serve to define for each department

Figure 9.1 Cycle of strategic goal attainment.

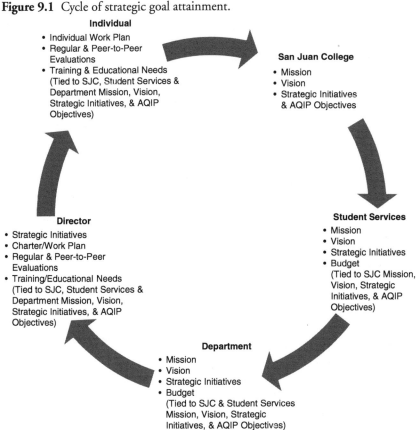

not only how its members will engage as service providers but also, and as important, how they will educate themselves and students in this overall college learning environment. As shown in Figure 9.1, the accreditation of the college is based on quality improvement processes as indicated by the Higher Learning Commission's Academic Quality Improvement Program (AQIP). The flow of the stated mission, vision, and strategies into the cycle created for student services follows these quality improvement processes.

The cycle continues as the strategic initiatives developed for the year are continued through the development of each employee's initiatives, which continue the articulated linkage back through the process of departmental, student services, and overall college goals and outcomes. The continuing need for review on an annual basis ensures that the linkages and overall alignment are current and that the outcomes indicated through the initiatives are on course for achievement of the college's goals.

The college's values play many roles in this entire process, but one of the most important is the recognition of each administrative, faculty, and student affairs/service member's contributions to the progress of college goal achievement and his or her respective role in that achievement. Members of an organization who do not understand how important their work is to the mission and goals feel less empowered and thus less productive than those who do. Leadership fully incorporates linkages of individual initiatives and performance to overall progress of the organization. This is important not only to the ability of an organization to change (Burke, 2008) but to the ability of the organization to have each employee aware of the role he or she plays and its relationship to the changes occurring within as well as outside the organization. Each stakeholder's awareness can be related to his or her own continual negotiation between the organization as it perceives itself and cultures (representing different staff perspectives) in alternative and sometimes opposing viewpoints, which allows for a broader view of the multiple interests in the environments that affect the organization (Bryson, 2008). This process allows for a far more dynamic and responsive organization with all members being empowered for its continuing success.

Programmatic Need for Learning Outcomes and Assessment

The need for a culture of change within student or academic services at a community or two-year college is further inherent if the organization desires to promote learning. At San Juan College, all staff must be "aware of the importance of taking account of the dynamics of individual and organizational learning as the necessary condition for organizational change" (Ruben, 2005, p. 382). The culture of learning as adopted by staff in student services in particular can then be extended to their acceptance of their role as not just deliverers of services but also educators.

Terry O'Banion (1997) presented theories on learning with the premise that a learning college provides education in a continual learning environment. San Juan College adopted his concept of a learning college more than a decade ago and continues to maintain it, as evidenced by its vision statement. Student services undertook to engage this culture of learning as core to the change it underwent and thus ensured that all staff members would understand and respect their active role in a learning environment. The need for understanding and acceptance of the principles of a "learning college" (O'Banion, 1997) was part of the education of staff in student services departments. The six principles of a learning college as articulated by O'Banion are

1. Creates substantive change in individual learners
2. Engages learners as full partners in the learning process
3. Creates and offers as many options for learning as possible

4. Assists learners to form and participate in collaborative learning activities
5. Defines roles of learning facilitators by the needs of the learners
6. Realizes success only when improved and expanded learning can be documented for its learners (1997, p. 47)

The O'Banion principles, which informed the development of the vision for San Juan College, create the framework for student learning and its assessment in student services and its departments. The word *learners* incorporated into the principles has provided a definition that student services can adhere to, because the traditional definition of *student* is not appropriate for some departments relative to their engagement in a learning college environment and an educator role. Affixing the title "learner" to members of any group that can be provided education greatly expands the educational scope of a college and provides greater impact and value to any community it serves.

These learning experiences, whether with traditional students or other types of learners, can be developed into a definite quantifiable method and appropriately assessed for learning achievement. The outcomes defined for student services and academic learning can be measured and, through that measurement, be reviewed for improvements. This assessment has additional needs because it becomes a substantiated indicator of student learning and development as a result of interactions with each department, which can be relayed to all constituencies providing funding or oversight for the college. O'Banion (1997) correctly indicates an institution-wide concern about student learning, and its assessment created the foundation for the concept of a learning college.

The continuance of student services involvement in the culture of institution-wide learning is affirmed by the college's vision. The case for a learning college based on assessment practices and measured outcomes only grows stronger as community and two-year college stakeholders and students rightfully demand more accountability as the cost of education rises.

Personnel Evaluations Incorporating Outcomes-Based Assessment and Program Initiative

The continuance of change for incorporation of a learning environment as articulated in the principles of a learning college (O'Banion, 1997) must be portrayed in the performance and the evaluation of that performance for each employee. The concept of quality process improvement, which the AQIP accreditation ascribes to, indicates that "employees have the opportunity to actively engage in continuous improvement activities. . . . Through increased communication and consultation, employees may feel a greater identification with, involvement in and loyalty to the organization" (Coyle-Shapiro, 1999, pp. 8–9).

Figure 9.2 Student services model for comprehensive employee performance.

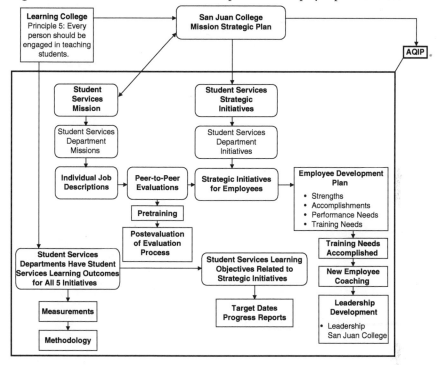

The professional and support staff assisted in the design of the performance methodology developed in student services. A continuing effort each year has been pretraining for all employees and postassessment of the evaluation process to ensure that the needs of the college, student services, and all staff members are being met. Figure 9.2 illustrates the student services model for comprehensive employee performance.

At San Juan College, performance evaluation is not a simple once-a-year task utilizing only prepackaged weighted criteria. The system developed by student services has a defined job description for the general requirements of each position. This is reviewed on an annual basis to ensure that it is current with position requirements. The annual review portion of the evaluation starts with the supervisor and the employee discussing the people internal and external to the campus who can best evaluate their performance over the past year. After concurrence on the peer evaluators, a message is sent to each with a statement from the vice president who articulates the reason for the evaluation and the need for candor and honesty. The criteria listed for professional staff are specific to them and in fact developed by them in previous workshops. A similar process is utilized for the support staff within student services departments. Each set of criteria undergoes a postevaluation work session to ascertain whether the criteria are still relevant and accurate in assessing work performance.

The actual review of the criteria-based performance is conducted in a discussion between the employee and the supervisor with averaged scoring from the peer group, employee scores, and supervisor scores compoising the evaluation material. The philosophy behind the discussion is to reach concurrence on the areas in the employee performance that are strong and to be congratulated, and the areas that indicate a need for improvement.

Prior to the review, the employee has worked individually and with his or her supervisor to develop the strategic initiatives to be worked on in the upcoming year. Care is taken to ensure that these initiatives are clearly linked to the student services and overall college initiatives, and anticipated timelines and documentable measures of completion are included. The student services learning objectives, which each department has undertaken, are included in the strategic initiatives for each employee. This year, in an ongoing effort to improve the model of evaluation, appropriate values engaged by the college will be correlated to individual strategic initiatives.

The performance review continues with discussion of the employee's contributions to the college and the positive effects of the employee's performance. The central part of the discussion then becomes the gaps in the employee's performance as identified by himself or herself, as well as by the employee's peers and supervisor, along with how these areas can be improved. Arriving at the strategies for improvement provides the impetus for an ongoing plan of training, education, and skill development needs to assist the employee in achieving that improvement.

Throughout the course of the year, the continual review of the plans agreed upon by employee and supervisor provides points of consideration in their regular meetings. This continuing review of all aspects of the performance plan allows assessment of initiative success and of the progress in achieving the college goal to which it is linked and the reallocation of resources. The college is currently evaluating the key performance indicators, which will ensure progress of the strategic goals approved by the board of trustees. As these indicators are finalized, the strategic initiatives and performance indicators of each employee will be reviewed to ensure their integration and to assign appropriate measures to them. This will also ensure continued integration of resource reallocation.

Because the college has adopted the model of student services performance evaluation for the entire institution, it is now undergoing transformation. A data system is being developed to incorporate the evaluation system in its entirety, and student services departments are conducting the pilot of the new program. Once completed, the system should allow easier tracking and management of all aspects of performance, easier integration of strategic initiatives to the overall college efforts, and monitoring of educational and training needs of each employee.

The learning assessment programs for each department and student services are being transformed into a data management system as well. This process will allow the departments to better manage the progress of each outcome they have identified for learning assessment as well as better integrate these results with performance. In turn, such a process will ensure a tighter alignment of resource allocation and reallocation for both academic and student services.

Performance and Program Needs for Budget Identification

The integration of budget planning and performance is reliant on the institutional budgeting process. The ability of an organization to adapt to change through planning and budgeting provides the basis for success in that endeavor. An institution must have, according to Garner (1991), "a strong set of accounting and budgeting systems, integrated from the beginning of the year to the end of the year and linked from the beginning of the life of the organization to the present" (p. xv). Garner goes on to explain that "the primary factor in public entities' ability to obtain funding is to demonstrate the resource allocations are being used efficiently and effectively" (p. 89). This translates into the need for performance and ensuing improvements in that performance to be measured as a precursor to budget requests.

As illustrated in Figure 9.1, budget planning occurs within departments as part of the overall annualized cycle. The development of initiatives has a corresponding role in departmental budget preparation. The identification of additional resources for implementation of initiatives or employee per-formance enhancements is part of the performance evaluation process. This information as well as the negation of resources as goals are completed should be extrapolated into the budget planning for each department as the budget planning cycle commences.

The inclusion of learning outcomes in each department's budget pre-paration process should be part of the strategic initiative identification and implementation process. The outcomes have their unique measurement and attainment processes but clearly are included in department planning and budgeting with the other strategies identified for resource allocation.

Once incorporated into overall institutional budgeting practices, the budget plan for each department, student services, and the college can then utilize a direct correlation for resource allocations to measurable out-comes, which are monitored through assessment for effectiveness and needed changes. This reinforces the learning college concept because evidence-based learning can be articulated through outcomes tied to resource allocation and evaluated employee performance improvements.

Foundational Questions for Institutions to Consider

Now that you have read the San Juan College example, you may be wondering how you can apply that model or its organizational learning directly to your own campus. The following set of questions will help you to identify the likelihood that your organization will be able to structurally support using outcomes-based program review results to prioritize resource allocations. Keep in mind that resource allocation decisions are made at various levels of the organization (course, program, department, college, institution, system, state, federal); thus, this discussion can be facilitated at any level within your organization.

1. Is your organizational leadership clear on what it values (on whatever level—functional area, program, department, college, institution—the resource decision is based)? Are the values prioritized?
2. Do you have goals and/or strategic initiatives articulated for the values that you have prioritized?
3. Are program and service leadership able to align their outcomes with the goals and strategic initiatives that your organizational leadership prioritizes?
4. Do your budgeting process and practice align with what your organizational leadership values?
5. Do your resource allocation process and practice align with what your organizational leadership values?

Implementation Questions

Once you have determined that a foundation for allocating resources based on evidence exists, the following questions can be used to implement the practice of (a) allocating resources to programs and services to maintain their quality or improve their quality, (b) choosing to eliminate programs and services, or (c) choosing to initiate new programs and services:

1. Which programs and services have outcomes that align directly with your organization's
   a. mission?
   b. vision?

    c. strategic initiatives for the present and future?

    d. values?

    e. priorities?

    f. goals?

2. Of the programs and services that align with your organizational values, which ones have gathered evidence to demonstrate that maintaining resources at the current level will potentially

    a. improve the quality of expected outcomes?

    b. decrease the quality of expected outcomes?

    c. maintain the current level of quality of expected outcomes?

3. Of the programs and services that align with your organizational values and have gathered evidence to demonstrate that maintaining resources at the current level will potentially improve the quality of expected outcomes, can you manage to maintain their current level of funding?

    a. If yes, then do so.

    b. If no, prioritize them to determine which ones may better fit with your organizational vision, preparing you for success in the present and the future, and allocate funds (at the same level or at an increased level or decreased level) according to their level of prioritization and your overall budget and capacity to do so.

4. Of the programs and services that align with your organizational values and have gathered evidence to demonstrate that maintaining resources at the current level will potentially decrease the quality of expected outcomes, can you manage to increase their current level of funding?

    a. If yes, then do so.

    b. If no, prioritize them to determine which ones may better fit with your organizational vision, preparing you for success in the present and the future, and allocate funds (at the same level or at an increased level or decreased level) according to their level of prioritization and your overall budget and capacity to do so.

5. Of the programs and services that align with your organizational values and have gathered evidence to demonstrate that maintaining resources at the current level will potentially maintain the quality of expected outcomes, can you manage to maintain their current level of funding?

    a. If yes, then do so.

    b. If no, prioritize them to determine which ones may better fit with your organizational vision, preparing you for success in the present and the future, and allocate funds (at the same level or at an increased level or decreased level) according to their level of prioritization and your overall budget and capacity to do so.

6. Group all the programs and services that are to receive the same allocation of funding as last year; what is the total?

7. Group all the programs and services that are to receive an increase in funding over last year; what is the total?

8. Group all the programs and services that are to receive a decrease in funding over last year; what is the total?

9. Can your budget cover the totals of the resources identified in questions 6–8? If not, move the lower prioritized programs for each category or for one category, depending on what your organization seeks to accomplish, into the category of programs and services discussed in question 10.

10. With the remaining groups (if there are still resources in the budget), determine which programs and services (that align with organizational values and with present and future strategic initiatives) to keep or which are necessary for the basic functioning of the organization (and for which it has been determined that outsourcing is not possible). Determine whether decreased quality of outcomes would be acceptable to the organizational leadership and constituents if those programs and services were cut or if funding were decreased. Then, make those very tough decisions and briefly explain why you made them.

Although it is understood that the aforementioned questions are simplistically presented and that many factors influence decision making other than evidence, the point of presenting these questions is to begin to implement transparent evidence-based allocation of resources on your own campus. With clearly articulated values and strategic priorities in which your organization is willing to invest and a prioritized manner in which they are funded, all constituents of your organization can make better decisions about where to invest their own energy and time. Everyone in the organization is thus empowered in a time when the economic crisis feels as if it has stripped organizations of all their humanity and compassion.

Finally, it is recognized that this chapter addresses the allocation of only those resources that align with organizational values and with present and future organizational strategic initiatives. Keep in mind that this resource allocation process can occur on every level of the organization and, therefore, some priorities may differ at various levels. As long as each level of the organization has authority over the manner in which it determines its values and priorities and is given resources to allocate, this process means that values and strategic priorities do not have to align all the way up the hierarchic organizational ladder unless the resource allocation and budgeting processes are designed to facilitate and expect such alignment.

Conclusion

While we illustrate the interplay of a comprehensive model of assessment, performance evaluation, and strategic planning in accordance with organizational values for one community college, we also highlight the challenges that occur in designing the planning processes because we are always operating within a context of continual change. Thus, this chapter has provided the reader with an overview of questions that will help leaders prioritize what is discovered from the outcomes-based assessment program review processes in a manner that will inform resource reallocations and ultimately influence effective strategic planning.

References

Bresciani, M. J., Gillig, B., Weiner, L., Tucker, M., & McCully, L. (Under Review). Exploring the use of evidence in resource allocation: Towards a conceptual framework for practice. *Research and Practice in Assessment Journal.*

Bresciani, M. J., Moore Gardner, M., & Hickmott, J. (2009). *Demonstrating student success: A practical guide to outcomes-based assessment of learning and development in student affairs.* Sterling, VA: Stylus.

Bryson, J. (2008). Dominant, emergent, and residual culture: The dynamics of organizational change. *Journal of Organizational Change Management, 21*(6), 743–757. doi:10.1108/09534810810915754

Burke, W. W. (2008). *Organization change: Theory and practice.* Thousand Oaks, CA: Sage.

Coyle-Shapiro, J. A.-M. (1999). Employee participation and assessment of an organizational change intervention: A three wave study of Total Quality Management. *Journal of Applied Behavioral Science, 35*(4), 439–456. Retrieved from http://eprints.lse.ac.uk/archive/00000835

Crowley, M. C. (2011). *Lead from the heart: Transformational leadership for the 21st century.* Bloomington, IN: Balboa Press.

Freeman, J., Bresciani, M. J., & Bresciani, D. L. (2004). *Integrated strategic planning: Bringing planning and assessment together.* Retrieved from http://www.naspa.org/membership/mem/pubs/nr/default.cfm?id=1327

Garner, C. W. (1991). *Accounting and budgeting in public and nonprofit organizations.* San Francisco, CA: Jossey-Bass.

Kouzes, J., & Posner, B. (2008). *The leadership challenge* (4th ed.). San Francisco, CA: Jossey-Bass.

O'Banion, T. (1997). *A learning college for the 21st century.* Phoenix, AZ: Oryx Press.

Rhoades, A. (2011). *Built on values: Creating an enviable culture that outperforms the competition.* San Francisco, CA: Jossey-Bass.

Ruben, B. D. (2005). The center for organizational development and leadership at Rutgers University: A case study, "Organizing Development and change in Universities." *Advances in Developing Human Resources, 7*(3), 368–395. doi:10.1077/1523422305277177

San Juan College. (2013a). *About SJC*. Retrieved from http://www. sanjuancollege .edu/pages/3533.asp

San Juan College. (2013b). *San Juan College strategic goals*. Retrieved from http:// www. sanjuancollege.edu/pages/6112.asp

Soparnot, R. (2011). The concept of organizational change capacity. *Journal of Organizational Change Management, 24*(5), 640–661. doi:10.1108/0953481 1111158903

van Eijnatten, F. M., & Putnik, G. D. (2004). Chaos, complexity, learning, and the learning organization: Towards a chaordic enterprise. *The Learning Organization, 11*(6), 418–429. doi:10.1108/09696470410548782

Wheatley, M. J. (2006). *Leadership and the new science*. San Francisco, CA: Berrett-Kohler.

10

EVALUATING THE PROCESS

Thomas C. Priester and Stacey N. Pierce

There is a sense of pride and relief that comes with the accomplishment of completing an assessment project, but like a good teacher at the conclusion of a lesson, you need to take that final step of intentionally reflecting on the process. The common-thread question is: What will I do differently next time? The question is affirmative rather than hypothetical because you will likely have the opportunity to complete an assessment project again.

The simple answer to the question of what you will do differently may very well be nothing. However, we all know that consistently doing something the same way will consistently lead to the same results. The community and two-year college environments are ever-changing with continual calls for accountability, competing priorities, and demands on resources (which are often limited). As a result, higher education practitioners at such institutions must be able to make decisions that are sound and informed. A good assessment process lays a strong foundation for sound and data-informed decision making.

I recall during my doctoral work a time when a wise professor in the program posed the idea that we (the doctoral students) were not learning about the thought anymore; we were now being challenged to actually think about the thought. Perhaps mind straining at first, this concept of deconstructing thought or digging deeper (and even deeper) to reveal the underlying meaning from where the thought emerged serves as a frame for this chapter on evaluating the process of assessment. The concept of thinking about the thought is analogous to assessing the assessment.

Much like the deconstruction of a house leaves exposed beams and the foundation that frame the structure, the deconstruction of the assessment process should leave exposed the institutional mission, vision, and goals that underpin your assessment efforts that foster an ever-evolving spirit of progress in student learning and services at every level of the community and two-year college: institutional, divisional, departmental, and programmatic all the way to the course level.

Food for Thought

Question: How do you know if your students are able to do what you say they can do?
Answer: You assess them.

Question: How do you know if your assessment process did what you said it would do?
Answer: You assess it.

At the conclusion of the assessment process, ask yourself and your team members: Did the data talk to us? What did the data say? How do the data speak to the future of our department? Then take it a step further and ask: What will we do differently the next time we collect data?

Consider the comments that you might hear while the assessment process is in full motion. You may hear (or even yourself utter) such statements as, "Let's keep that in mind for next time" or "It is what it is." In fact, community and two-year college employees might be most notorious for using such statements given the multitude of responsibilities and functional services that can sometimes be housed under a single department. While four-year colleges and universities may have an office (with a team of professional staff members) designated solely for functional programmatic areas such as new student orientation, leadership development, and volunteerism, these same programs may very well be delegated to a single office at a community or two-year college such as student life and are all overseen by a professional staff member such as a coordinator or director.

Where does that leave the assessment process? Even if you are the sole coordinator in an office responsible for a host of essential functions (as many professional staff members at community and two-year colleges are), you are not excused from the assessment cycle. Thus, the ability to take some liberties and be creative with your assessment process is essential. The key is to keep the goal in mind—strive to be involved in assessment efforts that help you understand the quality of your service, inform your decision-making process, and improve the services offered to students. In the following sections, we outline some thoughts on how assessors at community and two-year colleges may consider assessing the assessment process.

Mapping Out the Process

The assessment process may seem daunting to some. Some may fear it. Some may question it. Some just do not understand it. Much like a curriculum map provides a visual summation of where, when, and how student learning outcomes are assessed at an institution, an assessment process map can help to clarify where, when, and how the assessment process works from start to finish (Maki, 2002). Outline the roads to take to get to the final destination. Anticipate "roadblocks" and recalculate alternative pathways to stay on track toward the final destination (Bresciani, Moore Gardner, & Hickmott, 2009; Maki, 2002).

Mapping out your assessment process allows you to plan out your journey. When it comes to assessment, having a plan to guide your process is essential. A plan allows you to integrate the assessment process into your work, as opposed to adding it to the end of your to-do list and thinking of it as one more thing that has to get done. A mapped-out plan for assessment also helps you to be accountable to yourself and the assessment work that needs to get done: Write it down and do it! Remember to make your assessment process purposeful; plan to use the data; understand that assessment is not always perfect; and, most of all, keep it simple.

Consider Snyder's (2000) Hope Theory, which defines the concept of hope as the "sum of perceived capabilities to produce routes to desired goals, along with the perceived motivation to use those routes" (p. 8). The three core elements of Snyder's Hope Theory are (a) the conceptualization of a goal, (b) the developed routes to obtain the conceptualized goal (pathways), and (c) the motivation to obtain the conceptualized goal (agency).

Similarly, your assessment project contains the same components: a goal (better services), agency (a desire for continual improvement), and the pathway (process). Therefore, using the framework of Snyder's Hope Theory, your *assessment project* can be defined as the sum of your desire for continual improvement and process in order to deliver better services (see Figure 10.1). The equation for assessment is: Desire for Continual Improvement + Process = Better Services.

Hope does not exist without either element of agency/desire for better services or pathways/assessment process, and neither do your assessment projects. While your desire for continual improvement fosters motivation to achieve better services, multiple alternate processes may be (and arguably should be) available to attain the goal of better services. Therefore, when a hurdle causes a blockage in the original process to reach the desired goal, alternate assessment processes need to be explored.

Hopeful thinkers (or in this case hopeful assessors) are able to identify alternate pathways (processes) to channel their motivation (desire for

Figure 10.1 Hope-inspired assessment process map.

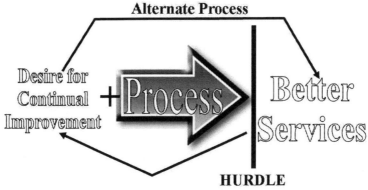

continual improvement) toward the desired goal (better services), whereas less hopeful thinkers might give up on the desired goal (better services). Figure 10.1 illustrates the placement of a hurdle in the hope-inspired assessment process map (right before the goal is reached) that causes recalculation of the motivation and identification of an alternate pathway to the desired goal (represented by the clockwise arrows).

Use the hope-inspired assessment process map as an evaluative tool when planning your assessment project. Clearly identify your goal for better services, and allow your goal to be directly driven by your desire for continual improvement. Then, consider the process (and the alternate processes) taken to achieve your goal. What happens if your original assessment project crashes and burns? Is there a plan B? How about a plan C?

Blogging About the Process

To keep the assessment of the assessment process purposeful, you must begin with the end in mind and evaluate the process while it is in motion. Compose a weekly narrative about the assessment process and broadcast it by sharing your thoughts with colleagues through a blog. Diplomatically journal about the process by writing about what is going well (and what is not going well) with the process. By providing a running dialogue, you may help to demystify the assessment process for colleagues. The assessment process should be as transparent as possible, and maintaining a blog will surely allow stakeholders (or perhaps even those who would like to learn more about the purpose of what you do and how you do it) to have an instant, working live update. Additionally, blogging about the assessment process will create an archive to use once the process is complete. Then, some simple coding could inform practice when it comes time to unveil the next assessment process. Invite others to follow and comment on your blog. Capture the "Let's keep this in mind for next time" moments so that they can be used when planning the next assessment process.

Blogging about your assessment process allows you to capture your journey in real time. By reviewing and analyzing this piece of the assessment process, you can identify timing conflicts or more optimal intervals during which you can engage in the assessment process. You may notice that you are heavily loaded at a particular time during the semester, or you may notice a downtime (a rarity in the community or two-year college environment) where it might be more sensible to conduct some of your assessment work. Often when we are in the midst of our work, it is difficult to recognize these opportunities. Taking the time to review the narrative of your process can be beneficial and help improve the quality of your assessment efforts.

Developing Outcomes and Creating a Rubric for the Process

What is the assessment process designed to do? In a highly unscientific Facebook survey, when asked what the characteristics of a good assessment process were, many colleagues who work in the field of education (middle school, high school, and higher) left comments such as "collaborative," "simple," "repeatable," "purposeful," "authentic," "open," "honest," and "clear." Begin with the end in mind and brainstorm what makes a good assessment process and use that information to construct a rubric. This is a clever method to document the effectiveness of the assessment process. What better way to assess your assessment process than to create a rubric to measure whether your assessment process was indeed (fill in the blank with the criteria that you develop for what you determine to be the characteristics of a good assessment process)?

For example, with a focus on the previously stated idea that a characteristic of a good assessment process is that it is collaborative, the author presents the following as a potential outcome:

> All seven professional staff members in the Office of Housing and Residential Life at State Community College will champion at least one aspect of the assessment process (e.g., benchmarking, developing an evaluation instrument, collecting data, analyzing data, synthesizing data, maintaining a blog, composing an executive summary/annual report).

Table 10.1 provides a rubric for this example.

TABLE 10.1

Sample rubric for assessment process of the Office of Housing and Residential Life at State Community College.

Characteristic	3	2	1	0	Comments
Collaborative	Seven professional staff members in the Office of Housing and Residential Life at State Community College championed at least one aspect of the assessment process.	Six professional staff members in the Office of Housing and Residential Life at State Community College championed at least one aspect of the assessment process.	Five professional staff members in the Office of Housing and Residential Life at State Community College championed at least one aspect of the assessment process.	Four or fewer professional staff members in the Office of Housing and Residential Life at State Community College championed at least one aspect of the assessment process.	

Conducting a SWOT Analysis of the Process of Assessment

A SWOT (strengths, weaknesses, opportunities, and threats) analysis may be used as an evaluation instrument. As part of the assessment process, this time, think about the thought and assess the assessment with an analysis of the actual process. The process of assessment has its own unique strengths, weaknesses, opportunities, and threats. Once the process is completed, take time to analyze the data collected through other evaluative instruments to analyze the positives, the challenges, the motivations, and the hurdles of your assessment process. A SWOT analysis will anchor the thoughts of those involved in your process and can be used as a springboard for the next assessment process.

Performing a SWOT analysis provides the opportunity to look at each portion of your assessment process and identify the strengths, weaknesses, opportunities, and threats. By engaging in this activity you can capitalize on strengths, address weaknesses (as best as you can given the resources and options available to you), take advantage of opportunities, and minimize the impact of threats to your assessment process. This is a critical part of your evaluation and planning in the ongoing cycle of assessment. If you simply repeat what you have done without the benefit of understanding what a SWOT analysis can highlight for you, you will likely overlook the opportunity to enhance the quality of your assessment efforts.

Case Study

Here is a real-world example that we use to frame this chapter. At State Community College, a housing and residence life program was implemented to support the college's goal of increasing its out-of-county and out-of state student demographic. Unlike students at many four-year colleges and universities, most community and two-year college students, like those at State CC, do not have a benchmark for what housing and residence life programs and those in the role of resident assistants (RAs) look like. It is generally true that community and two-year colleges tend to enroll more first-generation college students than four-year institutions (Laden, 2004; O'Banion, 2011).

When State CC implemented its housing and residence life program, it experienced a high rate of turnover among students in the RA role in the first year of the program's operation. The professional staff provided the RAs with a general training that most housing and residence life programs would view as typical. What State CC had not prepared for or anticipated was that students saw the role as a job, rather than a lifestyle, whereas most in the field would qualify it as the latter. Students expected to work set hours and then be done with the job. They did not understand or fully grasp that they were always operating in their role of creating community and being a resource to residents, looked to as a role model, and held to a higher standard of expectations. The professionals in the Office of Housing and Residential Life at State CC realized that they had some work to do if they were going to move the program forward and be successful.

The staff went back to the drawing board at the conclusion of their first academic year. That included looking at the feedback they had received from the RAs about the training they had received at the beginning of the fall and spring semesters. It was time for them to assess their assessment (they did not call it that, but we are cluing you into where this all starts to come together).

Strengths

The staff had collected feedback and input from the RAs about training that could be used to guide and inform changes made to the training going forward. The staff had feedback surveys from the RAs about the training they had received in the fall and spring. The staff had exit interviews with RAs who left the position or who were asked to vacate the position. The staff were aware that they needed to do something different, not for the sake of being different, but, rather, for the sake of providing quality and meaningful training to RAs that would prepare them for their role so that they could help the department reach its goals. Those goals were based on the CAS Self-Assessment Guide for Housing and Residential Life Programs (Council for the Advancement of Standards in Higher Education, 2012):

Part 4: Human Resources

- Student employees and volunteers must be carefully selected, trained, supervised, and evaluated. They must be educated on how and when to refer those in need of additional assistance to qualified staff members and must have access to a supervisor for assistance in making these judgments. Student employees and volunteers must be provided clear and precise job descriptions, pre-service training based on assessed needs, and continuing staff development.
- HRLP professional staff members must train resident/community assistants and other paraprofessionals to contribute to the accomplishment of the following functions: (a) community development (b) educational programming, (c) administration, (d) group and activity advising, (e) leadership development, (f) student conduct, (g) role modeling, (h) individual assistance and referral, (i) providing information, (j) crisis intervention, and (k) facilities management.
- All HRLP staff members, including student employees and volunteers, must receive specific training on institutional policies pertaining to functions or activities they support and to privacy and confidentiality policies and laws regarding access to student records and other sensitive institutional information. (Council for the Advancement of Standards in Higher Education, 2012, p.33)

Weaknesses

The staff first realized that they had not assessed what knowledge (or what lack of knowledge) the RAs had when they were hired for the position. This information could have been useful in helping them craft a training that would have been more beneficial to the inaugural RA staff. What the staff then noticed was that many of the RAs had noted in the feedback survey that at the end of the two-week training period they could not recall all of the sessions they had attended. Weaknesses identified in a SWOT analysis do not need to be numerous to prove impactful. State CC could attest to this statement.

Opportunities

State CC was able to identify several ways in which it could improve its assessment efforts as it prepared to train the next cohort of RAs. Implementation of a method that would allow the staff to assess the RAs' knowledge before they received any training and then again after they completed the training was noted as one of the first changes the staff would make. The staff also recognized the need to gather feedback immediately following each session. The use of learning outcomes to shape and drive the training sessions was also seen as an opportunity for improvement. The staff brainstormed the use of small-group review sessions at the end of each training day to further highlight training successes and deficiencies. Last, and perhaps the most impactful opportunity, was using information gathered during training to alter the training while in progress and to dictate training sessions that would take place during the year. Indeed, the opportunities were plentiful.

Threats

Addressing threats was perhaps the most difficult part of the process, but the staff knew they needed to be diligent in their work and not overlook this important area. An example of a threat, in this case, was the limited and fixed amount of training time.

When the staff finished the SWOT analysis process, they were hopeful that they could change their process and improve the outcome and also realized that the task ahead of them was not an easy one. However, they were dedicated to the process because they knew that in order to reach the goals of the department and to support the mission of the institution, they needed a well-trained, engaged, and motivated RA staff. The way to achieve this was through continual assessment of their practices. Their plan became to capitalize upon their strengths and transform opportunities into additional strengths. Then they would work to minimize weaknesses and remain aware of threats so they would not harm their progress.

Next Steps

Assessing your work is not hard but it is necessary. By taking the time to actively reflect upon and dissect your process, you can make changes that allow you to do it better the next time around. Using a SWOT analysis is a simple example of how this can be done easily whether you are an office of one or working with a larger team. But the work does not stop there. You will want to share your findings and get the information out to stakeholders across the institution and in some cases in your community. Keep reading to understand the importance of keeping your stakeholders informed.

Informing Stakeholders (Eliminating the Vacuum)

Once you have assessed the assessment, you want to clearly communicate your findings to your stakeholders focusing on the topics and areas of interest most pertinent to them (Bresciani et al., 2009; Maki, 2002). The information that the assessment process provides us is good for internal and external use. Because none of us work in a vacuum, it is likely that there are collaborators and supporters who will want to know about your findings. Perhaps they have ideas and insights that can help you reach new goals and achievements. Let us not forget about the potential for new relationships to be formed with other departments and offices that may not have been considered before. Remember, you do not want any blind spots. You want others to help you look at your findings and ask probing questions or offer ideas that you may not have considered. It is often those who are not involved in the kind of work we do daily who cause us to explain our work in a more thoughtful manner than we would have on our own. These explanations can lead to "aha" moments that can guide us further.

Take your results and go out and make others aware of what you have found. Be confident but be prepared to receive feedback and criticism. Not every encounter will be unicorns and rainbows, but we must remain focused on the goal at hand: to gain feedback that moves us forward. We acknowledge that it can be uncomfortable to place ourselves in a position where our work can be openly criticized by others. Therefore, keep the ideas on the process central to the conversation, and do not allow it to become personal. It is not about you; rather, it is about the work and its impact on those whom you serve.

Forgetting the Pretty Binders

Pretty binders of data collecting dust on the shelf do not do anyone any good, especially you (or your department, for that matter). How many of us have these binders full of information that we do not use or plan to use sitting on our shelves? As Schuh and Upcraft (2000) state, "Too often, assessment studies are given initial attention and then forgotten, or are roundly criticized as hopelessly flawed and dismissed, or suffer the ultimate ignominy: being ignored completely" (p. 14). This is exactly what you do not want to happen to your assessment results.

You should not collect data for the sake of collecting it (Bresciani et al., 2009; Maki, 2002; Schuh & Upcraft, 2000). That is a waste of time, energy, and resources, and because most of us already find these to be in short supply, it benefits us to be good stewards. Once you have the data, put it into action. Use the data to inform your processes, procedures, and practices. Use your assessment findings to drive conversations with your team and those who support your department, with whom you collaborate, or with whom you would like to form new relationships. Let these conversations stimulate the next steps for your organization and be the basis upon which good, informed decisions are made. Finally, allow your current assessment outcomes to help you plan for your next round of assessment because assessment should be occurring continually.

Conclusion

We all need to deconstruct our assessment houses on a regular basis. These purposeful and intentional looks at our practices and processes provide us with the opportunity to perform quality assessment. Beyond that we can examine our assessment methods to refine our efforts so that we are making effective decisions. There are simple, yet useful, strategies that academic and student affairs/services professionals can use to guide them through the process of evaluating their assessment processes, including the use of maps, blogs, rubrics, and SWOT analysis. The key is to begin somewhere and not allow yourself to be so bogged down in minutiae that you forget to take the time to do the work. The goal is to be ready for the next round so that you can improve assessment practices and enhance both your work and the overall student learning experience.

References

Bresciani, M. J., Moore Gardner, M., & Hickmott, J. (2009). *Demonstrating student success in student affairs.* Sterling, VA: Stylus.

Council for the Advancement of Standards in Higher Education. (2012). *CAS professional standards for higher education* (8th ed.).Washington, DC: Author.

Laden, B. V. (2004). Serving emerging majority students. In B. V. Laden (Ed.), *Serving minority populations.* New Directions for Community Colleges, 2004: 5–9. San Francisco, CA: Jossey-Bass.

Maki, P. L. (2002). Developing an assessment plan to learn about student learning. *Journal of Academic Librarianship, 28*(1/2), 8–13. doi:10.1016/S0099-1333(01)00295-6

O'Banion, T. (2011). Pathways to completion: Guidelines to boosting student success. *Community College Journal, 82*(1), 28–34.

Schuh, J. H., & Upcraft, M. L. (2000). Assessment politics. *About Campus, 5*(4), 14–21.

Snyder, C. (2000). *Handbook of hope: Theory, measures, and applications.* San Diego, CA: Academic Press.

11

LOOKING AHEAD

Moving Toward a More Holistic Approach to Assessment

Marilee J. Bresciani, John L. Hoffman, Jill Baker,
and Julianna Barnes

The Student Learning Imperative (American College Personnel Association, 1994) had quite an influence on my (Marilee Bresciani's) perception of a student affairs professional's role in students' learning and development. It was published when I was completing my doctoral research—the time when I was being trained to dissect every thought, word, and action in higher education. Just as I was learning about the intricacies and specialization of every aspect of higher education, I was also beginning to be challenged about reintegrating it all into a sense of oneness. Ironic? Perhaps not.

When I had the privilege of receiving my PhD in 1995, I was focused on proving to the world that I, the first in a long generational line to receive a PhD, was worthy of it. To make a long story short, in an effort to satisfy Ego above all else, I began to privilege the intellectual aspect of myself ignoring all the wisdom contained within the challenges of *The Student Learning Imperative*—within the wisdom of integrating all aspects of the Self, of the discovery of the Self, into the learning journey. Now, nearly 20 years later and after having had the privilege of meeting neuroscientists and quantum physicists, after having explored several inquiry avenues into the dissection of identifying where within the biological and chemical self is the evidence for how the Self learns and develops, I arrive here. Here, I share that we in higher education (biologically and chemically) cannot, at this point in time with the instrumentation that we have, discern the places of origin of the affect from those of the cognitive, emotions from thoughts, or past memories from the present moment experience; we can identify—to some extent—where they are all processed, but not where they originate. Therefore, why do we as educators and administrators try to make such distinctions between affect and cognition in our student learning and development assessment work?

I was drawn into the higher education profession because I saw a higher education system that was not aware that it was designed to advance the whole of human potential. To me, the student affairs profession existed to remind faculty and system leaders that they were to be about educating a whole person, not an isolated intellect, or a mental illness, or a data point on a spreadsheet. In educating the whole of a human, that meant facilitating the human being to engage in the most exciting adventure of all: discovering who the authentic self is and determining whom she is in relationship to everything else that she may encounter. Some of this can be "measured," but other parts cannot be measured because of our limited ability to do so.

If we toss out our commitment to intentionally designing and evaluating all systems as they relate to the facilitation of holistic student learning and development, then it is my humble opinion that we have lost the very essence of why we engage in assessment in the first place. I do not believe we are able to assess everything we do. I do believe we can become more committed to articulating how the intention (the outcomes) of everything we do exists to facilitate or support whole-person education and development. I believe we should allow the research that informs holistic or integrated student learning and development to drive the way in which we organize ourselves and deliver our services and curriculum. If we cannot articulate why what we do advances the wholeness of the human experience in education, then what exactly is our purpose and how will assessment inform that conversation?

It is from this place that I invited three colleagues of mine—two of whom are community college practitioners and one a longtime friend and exceptional scholar (all three exemplary *educational leaders*)—to join me in discourse, reflection, and the design of this chapter, which is intended to explore a more holistic approach to assessing student learning and development within community and two-year college student support and academic services. In our dialogue, we found ourselves facing the need to deconstruct many of our current practices in order to pursue our future purposes. Thus, while we touch on some of the issues that we see coming around the corner, we do so in the context of a call to a renewed focus on the whole student, a concept that lies at both the genesis of the community and two-year college movement and the four-year student affairs profession within the United States.

Framing Assessment Practice

It has been more than 20 years since Lee Bolman and Terrance Deal published the first edition of *Reframing Organizations: Artistry, Choice, and Leadership.* Through that book and the subsequent editions, Bolman and Deal (1991, 1997, 2003, 2008) have presented four frames around which they have synthesized organizational theory literature. From this basis, they then have made the case for leadership that draws upon each of the frames. The first of the four frames is the *structural,* which emphasizes organizational goals and objectives, the division of labor, and rational processes of analysis and restructuring to achieve change. Much of what we do in the assessment realm fits squarely within this frame. The second frame, *human resources,* emphasizes the relationships between organizations and people as well as the role of human motivation. Though this frame has received less attention within assessment circles, our experience is that many student affairs professionals are drawn to this way of viewing and understanding organizations. Bolman and Deal's third frame, the *political* frame, is fundamentally concerned with the allocation of scarce resources. This is certainly a concern for assessment-minded professionals, though our approach is typically more structural as we aim to use rational analytic processes to inform resourcing decisions. In contrast, the political frame considers how power, conflict, enduring differences, and the formation of coalitions drive those decisions. Finally, the *symbolic* frame assumes that developing meaning within the context of ambiguity as well as using myth, rituals, and ceremonies to shape organizational meaning is central to the understanding and leadership of organizations. Many assessment writers have discussed the importance of creating a "culture of assessment" within educational institutions (e.g., Bresciani, 2002; Callahan, 2008), but fewer discussions have utilized a symbolic frame approach as a means for accomplishing this culture.

A significant contribution of Bolman and Deal's four frames is their ability to help leaders identify and deconstruct their epistemological assumptions—their core beliefs and understandings of what organizations are and how they function. In the West, the structural is familiar and intuitive to most leaders; thus, discussions of organizational change often privilege structural perspectives. Consider, for example, how most planning processes utilize hierarchies of strategies, goals, and outcomes coupled with quantitative analyses that aim to identify organizational problems and solve them with policies, protocols, and reorganization. Likewise, most assessment models rely primarily on hierarchies of learning goals, objectives, and outcomes along with analyses that divide student growth into learning and development or cognition and affect. It is somewhat ironic that scientific studies of the brain have discovered that these types of dissections are inconsistent with brain functioning: The brain cannot distinguish between learning and development. The structural frame has value, but overreliance on the structural hides other important aspects of organizations.

Despite numerous scientific discoveries, most Western educators and educational leaders continue to privilege structural ways of knowing over other forms. It is interesting to note that early organizational theorists drew heavily on structural assumptions even as they laid out the foundations for the human resources (e.g., Barnard, 1938), political (e.g., Cyert & March, 1959), and symbolic (e.g., Argyris, Putnam, & Smith, 1985) frames. Extending beyond Bolman and Deal's frames, Scheurich and Young (1997) have argued that the assumptions made about the definitions of *research* and *validity* privilege Western ways of knowing over those of diverse cultural groups. Yet community and two-year colleges arguably educate the most diverse students in the world—students who bring diverse strengths, worldviews, and forms of cultural wealth to our campuses (see Yosso, 2005). If our assessment work is to become more holistic and more inclusive of the worldviews of the students whom we serve, we must generate new approaches that are more holistic and inclusive of other frames and diverse ways of knowing and being—even if we do not exactly know how to readily assess all aspects of that knowing and being.

Consider, for example, the very concept of outcomes. Although consistent in concept, the definition and scope of *outcomes* varies by college culture and is typically unique to each campus (Bergquist & Pawlak, 2008; Kezar & Eckel, 2002). Even within a structural framework, there is no one-size-fits-all solution or definition for *outcomes*. The leadership imperative, from a multiframe perspective, is not to narrow in on the establishment of a common definition of *outcomes*, but to move forward the dialogue regarding the deeper roles and purposes of outcomes and of education. Will outcomes assessment remain a checklist for compliance and little else? Will a more externally driven, draconian reality emerge where outcomes, made up of isolated data points often gathered through courses or larger institutional data sets, assume decision making for institutions? Or, will institutions look to actualize what *could be* with a fully holistic, integrated paradigm that best serves the student and ultimately all stakeholders? And, if the latter, how might that emerge? Consider a quick reframing of outcomes. From a human resources perspective, outcomes might be concerned less with what students will be able to know or do and more with how students (or faculty and staff) engage in relationships with college and community members. Additionally, outcomes influenced by a human resources perspective may do more to emphasize human needs, desires, and motivations. Politically, outcomes are scarce resources that power brokers use in negotiations. Note, for example, the controversies that have occurred regarding outcomes related to multicultural competence, human sexuality, or the educational canon. From a symbolic perspective, outcomes may have less to do with content and more to do with perception and meaning. If we extend the prior example, a multicultural outcome may validate the value and voice of some students on campus whereas others may perceive it to be an effort of the liberal academy to be politically correct. In both cases, these perceptions may emerge regardless of the intent, design, or content of the outcome, and perceptions will, in turn, influence holistic learning. We can evaluate the extent that members of a college community can regulate their emotions in order to promote peaceful and effective discourse. But we first have to instill these kinds of teachings into the fabric of every classroom and out-of-classroom environment; we have to become more committed to designing and then evaluating a complete student success curriculum.

A Holistic, Multiframe Approach to Assessment

In looking to advance a more fully integrated holistic model of education and assessment of its outcomes, some basic assumptions must be made. We assume, for example, that the locus for expressing and assessing learning outcomes is at the heart of all assessment work in which each division of the college is engaged according to its function and culture. To presume an integrated holistic approach, all pieces must align and fit together in a seamless fashion, and this includes across divisions, each with their own vocabularies and ways of doing, and across a campus structure, often with its own limitations. And, of course, a paradigm based on the whole person and his learning outcomes must be consistent with local culture, with its mission, vision, values, and goals (Bresciani, 2006; Schein, 2004).

With these assumptions of such a system met, one is limited only by imagination in proposing the next step in student learning assessment at the community college level. Nationally, we have multiple types of program review that are used according to purpose (Bers, 2011; Bresciani, 2006), but one integrating the whole person is not common. What is proposed here is a departure from past practice and an introduction of a model in which all pieces are tightly intertwined. At the center of student learning is the whole student, surrounded by the student's accomplishments in specific areas (see Figure 11.1). This is a far better picture of what the program and institution have achieved in terms of effecting change in the student's life and learning experience.

The challenge then becomes one of integration and assessment. How can this be measured and reported through an integrated means? How can one measure the level of integration? How can programs fully leverage it

Figure 11.1 Composite of student learning assessment for program review.

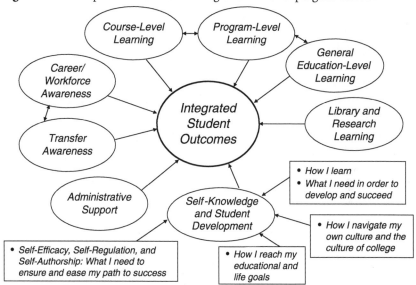

within their program reviews to inform planning and facilitate resource allocation? Dowd (2005) stated that in using data for assessment, it must be used to inform planning, not drive it; that it must be carefully defined and measured to serve the inquiry agendas of practitioners. The concept of data-driven decisions aligns with Bolman and Deal's structural frame, and it allows leaders to delegate decision making to the data and data analysis. However, a multiframe approach to leadership requires individuals in leadership to also consider human, political, and symbolic aspects when making decisions. Assessment data retain an important role in this process, but they also yield their privileged position to leaders who must consider multiple ways of organizational knowing and being when making decisions. Leaders make decisions that are informed not only by data but also by relationships, motivation, power dynamics, and meaning as well as by experience, consultation, and intuition.

Galbraith (2006) pointed out the need to align comprehensive strategy with structure, and that would be one of the biggest challenges in a move such as this (Bolman & Deal, 2008). How would one get it all to work together in a system currently in silos? In essence, getting it "all to work together" in the context of a multiframe approach would conceptually move beyond the structural frame or "metrics." As such, how could the different divisions—which may use different metrics—learn to speak each other's languages? Many change models call for the close attention to culture in any change effort, and especially one as massive as this (Beer, Eisenstat, & Spector, 1990; Kezar & Eckel, 2002; Kotter, 1995; Schein, 2004, 2006; Smart, Kuh, & Tierney, 1997). By definition, culture change is transformational change, and that is not easily achieved. But it begins by establishing trust in communication; therefore, it begins with individuals taking responsibility for their own attention, emotion, and cognitive regulation, which, thanks to neuroscience research, we now know is possible for anyone at any adult age (Alvarez & Emory, 2006; Bush, Luu, & Posner, 2000; Chan, Shum, Toulopoulou, & Chen, 2008; Chiesa, Calati, & Serretti, 2011; P. R. Goldin & Gross, 2010; Hölzel et al., 2007; Hölzel et al., 2008; Hölzel et al., 2011; Hutcherson, Goldin, Ramel, McRae, & Gross, 2008; Kozasa et al., 2012; Lazar et al., 2005; Lutz, Slagter, Dunne, & Davidson, 2008; and Todd, Cunningham, Anderson, & Thompson, 2012).

We have seen some progress in the integrative *delivery* of support services and curriculum, with learning communities one of the models du jour. An integrative *assessment* model, however, largely continues to evade us. To advance this agenda, leaders have to identify where the silos lie within their institutions and then embark upon the relentless work of creating bridges between them. Interestingly, we continue to refer to the major functions of our colleges as "divisions" (student services, instruction, and administrative services), language that is highly structural and that perhaps contributes to the perpetuation of the siloed status quo. Indeed, bridging the assessment gap between divisions, within divisions (e.g., counseling, admissions and records, financial aid), and even within a single department or program is an important step in facilitating progress toward holistic assessment. In speaking of the latter, for example, assessment cannot be solely the responsibility of the department chair or coordinator. Student learning and development, and the way we assess it, must be everyone's business, and it is important for all key constituents—administrators, faculty, staff, and students—to engage in this important work. Not only is broad engagement good practice, but inclusion of representatives from all governance groups in moving the agenda contributes to the likelihood of multiframe design and implementation. Equally important is the need for a profound understanding of the role that each plays in facilitating student learning and development. We continue to encourage community college leadership not to underestimate the role of classified staff members in assessment because they are often primary front-line practitioners with whom students interface within the institution.

With all of this said, a holistic integrated model for student learning would be challenging, and yet, it could be envisioned. To achieve this vision, a model that is developed locally to be consistent with college culture (Bergquist & Pawlak, 2008; Kezar & Eckel, 2002; Schein, 2004; Smart et al., 1997) could be constructed around the four frames of the organization identified by Bolman and Deal (2008). Figure 11.2 depicts a Venn diagram (admittedly a rather structural technique) presenting this interaction.

Figure 11.2 Program review: Visioning a holistic and integrated process using Bolman and Deal's four frames.

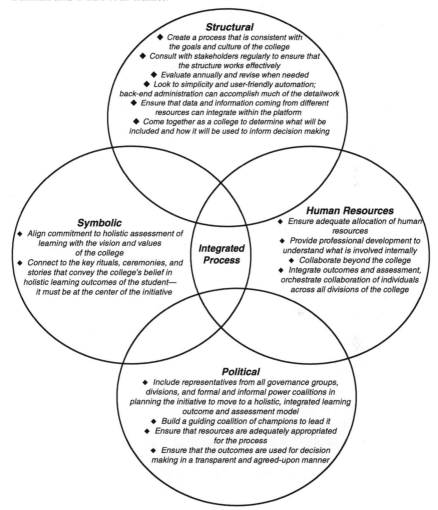

The question becomes one of leadership: getting from here to there. We know that change requires the direct and strong commitment of the executive staff, including the chief executive officer (Beer et al., 1990; Kezar & Eckel, 2002; Kotter, 1995; Schein, 2004). Further, theorists such as Kezar and Eckel (2002) developed frameworks for approaching change that are inclusive of the work of leaders across institutions. Institutions need leaders whose work can extend beyond mere structural and strategic planning or political negotiating and posturing. To this end, Hoffman (2010) suggested that leaders consider not only the metaphor of vision (Where are we going and how will we get there?), but also the metaphor of voice (Who are we, what do we value, and how do we speak to our present realities?). This perspective, grounded in humanistic and existential psychology, is consistent with human resources and symbolic frame perspectives. The hard work is for the college's leadership to make the commitment to foster holistic institutional identities in the here and now as well as engage in practices to shape and move toward a more comprehensive future. In the following sections, we consider several emergent and coming trends in assessment as related to the perspectives we have outlined thus far.

Moving Forward

Given the calls for further accountability, the emerging presence of Massive Open Online Courses (MOOCs), and the reality that revenues for education will likely remain precariously low, we know that community and two-year colleges are at a significant crossroads. Economic recovery, the further advancement of the economy, and the actualization of human potential depend on strong outcomes (Carnevale & Desrochers, 2004; C. Goldin & Katz, 2007). It is a perfect time to engage in deep questions such as: What outcomes do community and two-year colleges deliver and how well are they organized to deliver those outcomes? How well are community and two-year colleges designing and delivering holistic student learning and development?

In many cases, community and two-year college leadership has conformed to the letter, if not always the spirit, of mandated outcomes assessment, and this begs the question of outcome. Specifically, what is meant by "outcome"; what are its implications for the student and the stakeholders of that student's education; and does it inform a larger set of practices, such as both programwide and collegewide planning and decision making (Bresciani, 2006; Dowd, 2005)? Does it inform college-, district-, and statewide policy decisions? These questions underlie the frameworks we have discussed thus far, and they serve as an important context for the issues and trends that we discuss in this section of the chapter. They also provide us with an opportunity to become more focused and intentional in what we do; they provide an opportunity to prioritize.

Rejecting the Notion of Doing More With Less

If you have not been asked to do more with less in the past several years, you likely have not worked at a community or two-year college. But, what does it really mean to do more with less? As is the case with most institutions of the scale and scope of community and two-year colleges, there have been abuses where professionals have not been good stewards of the resources entrusted to them. In that sense, doing more with less simply translates as efficiency.

That said, characterizations of the community and two-year college sector as "fatty" or inefficient are misguided at best. So why do we repeatedly hear the expectation to do more with less? Some might suggest that it is simply the new normal. Fewer dollars are being invested in community and two-year colleges but the leadership is expected to serve increasing numbers of students, serve higher proportions of underprepared students, and produce more completers (e.g., graduates and transfers) in a shortened amount of time. We acknowledge these realities. In fact, we anticipate that these realities will reach new heights in the coming years, or in the very least, we will be required to offer services fully online and possibly even for free to align with the growing popularity of MOOCs. Yet, we also suggest that *doing more with less* is not a recipe for sustainable success in the long term. The reality of changes in funding must lead to changes in both *what* we do and *how* we do it. That is where a holistic approach to assessment comes in, and it begins with prioritizing what the organization values through collaborative conversations among all the organizational constituents and moves through the recognition that a community and two-year college education is much more than knowledge acquisition.

Assessment should inform *what* we do and assessment, coupled with the wealth of research we have at our fingertips, should inform how we do it. Too often, leaders abdicate their responsibility by responding to smaller budgets with across-the-board cuts paired with admonishments to do more with less. We have seen across the country that the majority of cuts are with regard to all that we understand research tells us are effective ways to design, deliver, and evaluate holistic learning and development. These leaders shift the blame, citing forces beyond their control; yet, as Hoffman (2010) has noted, the association of leadership with control is fallacy. Managers may, to a limited degree, be able to "control" small, closed systems. Leaders, however, must work within open systems that are more complex and ambiguous; those who wish to *control* are not leaders. Hoffman (2010) suggests that leaders can counter control instincts (we regard this as self-serving Ego or, from a cognitive neuroscience perspective, the need to survive at all costs) by focusing on organizational dignity, meaning, and voice, concepts that draw upon Bolman and Deal's (2008) human resources and symbolic frames. In the face of diminishing resources, this entails considering assessment data (along with intuition, theory, experience, the ever-growing constant of uncertainty and consultation) in order to make difficult decisions about the prioritization of funding allocations. Instead of trying to do more of every activity with fewer resources, some activities will need to be scaled down, completely redesigned, or even discontinued. Dignifying the work of employees who are also coeducators within community and two-year colleges means allowing (or requiring) them to stop doing all of their current work with fewer resources and inviting (or requiring) them to refocus on a smaller set of activities that can be done with the available resources and with dignity. In the end, having less may mean doing less, or it may mean doing "less" really well, which then brings on the appearance of doing more because our doing becomes an evidence-based, reflectively informed, and intentional way of being and doing.

Assessment should also inform *how* we do what we do. Developmental learning theory may present an additional perspective regarding how we do what we do. Jarvis (1987) described how some problems create a sense of disjuncture—tension, crisis—that contributes to changed cognitive, emotional, or behavioral actions and a new state of learning and development. Consider the adage to work smarter, not harder. Here, working smarter involves a developmental shift in the person; however, few of our current assessment practices yield data that can inform these types of shifts. Our experience has been that most closing-the-loop examples consist of changes in the design of educational programs rather than in the knowledge, skills, and motivations of the educators who enact those programs. Yet, Clark and Estes (2002) have suggested that securing meaningful change results from research and evaluation requires the consideration of knowledge, skills, and motivation as well as organizational systems. Early assessment implementation practices were careful to distinguish assessment from performance review in order to assuage potential resistance. Thus, most current assessment practices yield data that do not inform necessary professional development for faculty and staff (e.g., other means of working smarter).

Many institutions have long utilized student evaluations of teaching. These evaluations typically do not assess student learning, but if constructed well, they do gather data that can inform teaching practice and the engagement of the instructor with the student. For example, student responses to questions about the knowledge and preparation of the instructor, the teacher's ability to explain difficult concepts, or the faculty member's attentiveness to diverse learning styles may inform not only the design of the course curriculum but also the teacher's pedagogy. Some may pause here to note that these types of data border on measures of satisfaction rather than of learning. However, these types of questions are in actuality evaluating students' perceptions of the engagement of the instructor with them in the classroom. In addition, we invite community and two-year colleges to ask students to self-assess their level of engagement. Asking students to self-reflect on questions such as "How often did I complete the assigned readings prior to class" or "How often did I seek assistance outside of the class from a peer, a staff member, or an instructor" returns the conversation to the nature of the collaborative type of learning we are encouraging. The reality is that a holistic perspective of assessment involves collecting data about learning and mutual engagement as well as about involvement. To work smarter, educators need holistic data addressing how students learn, how they seek involvement, and how they engage with faculty and staff so that they can use this information to inform changes in their professional development (knowledge, skills, and motivation) plans as well as changes in programmatic design.

Narrow Versus Integrative Measures

Few stakeholder groups have the will or time to develop an in-depth, nuanced understanding of the community and two-year college. We simply cannot be experts in everything within today's information-rich society, and as such, we have trained ourselves to make decisions based on sound bites. For example, we make decisions about restaurants and hotels based on a five-star rating system, not knowing the criteria that informed the awarding of the stars; about movies based on a thumbs-up or thumbs-down (or possibly ripe versus rotten tomatoes); about cars based on miles per gallon; and about hospitals based on rankings and report cards. In this context, evaluations regarding the quality of elementary and secondary schools based on scores such as California's Academic Performance Index, which ranges from 200 to 1,000, seem quite sophisticated, even though we still are uncertain of the criteria that inform such an index, how those criteria were assembled, and what was overlooked.

We should not be surprised when stakeholders continue to evaluate the quality of a community college based primarily on its completion or transfer rate. Still, given the complexities of the multiple missions of community and two-year colleges as well as the diversity of our institutions, we know that these rating systems are not sufficient to inform students and other stakeholders of the quality of our institutions. Taken alone, they are certainly far from sufficient to inform continuing efforts to improve the quality of the education that we provide. How then do we design assessment and program review processes that can respond to the demands of accrediting agencies, meet the needs of students and their families, assist in our efforts to negotiate for limited institutional resources, and meaningfully inform the decisions we make as educators committed to excellence? Further, how do we do this in a manner that is sustainable over time and that honors the principles of brevity, simplicity, and practicality?

When consulting with community and two-year colleges and serving as external reviewers, we are encouraged to see progress in the articulation of student services learning outcomes that align with the broader institutional learning outcomes. At leading institutions, we now see examples of outcomes that are coupled with the collection and analysis of assessment data that lead to example "closing-the-loop" practices and practices that are aligned to promote institutional strategic initiatives. While we commend these practices, we also observe an opportunity for improvement with regard to the following:

- A realistic awareness of the capacity to serve the constituents in the manner intended with the resources provided
- Prioritization of strategic initiatives that continue to contribute to the notion of doing more with less
- Reallocation of resources to improve the strategic initiatives of an organization if they have been prioritized
- The ability to align meaningful outcomes-based assessment data and the decisions made with those data with performance indicators used by legislators
- Collaborative conversations that outline the needs for specific types of professional development for staff and instructors
- Collaborative conversations around what may be missing from the data gathered or the way in which we design and deliver learning and development and whether that is acceptable given what we do and do not know about holistic learning and development

In summarizing collaborative prioritization of resource reallocation, we return to the consideration of the frames. In terms of human resources, the integrated process we are proposing has the potential to engage multiple individuals in the collection of data related to a small set of broader learning objectives. Decisions about how to interpret and use these data to inform decisions will be less likely centered in the work of a single individual and more likely to draw together multiple professionals. This type of practice is thus more likely to reinforce the relationship among instructors, staff, and administrators as well as their motivation for engaging in assessment practices. Politically, large sets of discrete outcomes, assessment data, and recommendations pit individual practitioners against one another because each individual has data to support his or her claim for additional resources. This process will not eliminate the scarcity of resources or the realities of conflict within organizations, but it may be helpful in managing coalitions and focusing their attention on broader program-level objectives. Finally, in terms of the symbolic frame, a shared conceptual framework organized around three to five broader learning objectives has the potential to serve as a source of shared meaning. Because discrete outcomes are written for specific activities and compiled around shared objectives, the process addresses the routine activities of practitioners involved with the program, thus reinforcing their dispositions and professional habits.

What about the stakeholders? Let's return for a moment to the rating of one to five stars used to make a decision about a hotel stay. At first, a traveler may limit the number of choices based on overall star ratings, but when narrowing the list to a final choice, he or she may dig deeper to explore multiple additional ratings for cleanliness, service, facilities, and customer reviews. Not only do those extra ratings provide additional information about the hotel, but they serve to inform the customer about how one could or should make decisions regarding where to stay. The same is true here. Community and two-year colleges will be required by legislators to continue to provide information about graduation and transfer rates, but the approach outlined here allows educational leaders to provide context about what those numbers mean as well as additional information that may teach stakeholders how to make decisions about an institution's quality of education in a holistic manner.

Revisiting the Future of Accountability

An important step in advancing the holistic assessment agenda is for leadership to engage key institutional stakeholders in taking stock of where the institution is and where it wishes to be, with particular care given to being authentic about its current state. After all, if we are not able to be genuine about where we are, how are we ever going to take steps forward in a meaningful way? For some, the current focus may be at the technical "how-to" level, whereby the institution may be grappling with developing well-constructed student learning outcomes statements and ways to assess them, perhaps only sporadically throughout the institution. Other institutions may find that although they are engaged in more systematic, integrated processes of assessment, they may be so entrapped in the structural aspects of assessment that they fail to take the next important step: broad-scale dialogue. Engaging in broad-scale discussions across the institution takes us closer to a multiframe approach and can bring about the holistic improvements in student learning and development that brought us to engage in assessment in the first place.

Another aspect of holistic student learning and development assessment conversations is that for many colleges assessment is done only for accountability purposes (Bresciani, 2006; Brock et al., 2007). It is forced upon them by external agencies such as accrediting bodies and the federal government. It was discovered in 1997 (Roueche, Johnson, & Roueche, 1997) that most colleges did not use institutional effectiveness data required for external reporting in any significant manner for local applications. Many colleges continue to struggle to make this connection and leverage outcomes assessment for local application. However, some are now accomplishing it for purposes of integrated planning, ironically as a result of pressure from accrediting bodies. And this discussion is taking place all at a time when regional accreditation bodies may give way to state-mandated testing.

Testing

Educational policymakers have devoted significant attention to testing as a means of assessing student learning as well as of promoting greater accountability among higher education institutions. There is a strong body of literature documenting bias within standardized tests (Jencks & Phillips, 1998). These studies suggest that students of color, English-language learners, and students from low socioeconomic backgrounds tend to score lower on standardized tests regardless of their ability. Additionally, studies by Fleming (2002), Fleming and Garcia (1998), Hoffman (2002), and Hoffman and Lowitzki (2005) suggest that standardized tests may be better predictors of student success when students attend colleges and universities where the institutional culture is highly similar to the culture of their home and prior educational environments. As we consider most community college students—likely the first who will be required to complete tests as a prerequisite for a certificate or degree—it is evident that they are among those students for whom standardized tests are the least reliable or valid. Add many educators' resistance to being evaluated by test results (though we often use tests to evaluate our students), it is not surprising that so many educators are arguing against mandated testing, particularly when testing moves us further away from a return to holistic learning and development.

These arguments may have slowed the adoption and implementation of testing, yet we remain concerned that these arguments will continue. Thus, we cannot emphasize enough the need for instructors, staff, and administrators to come together to do the following:

- Prioritize strategic initiatives.
- Realistically assess the capacity to meet the strategic initiatives by serving their constituents in the manner intended with the resources provided.
- Reallocate resources to improve the strategic initiatives using outcomes-based assessment data.
- Align meaningful outcomes-based assessment data and the decisions made with those data with performance indicators used by legislators.
- Engage in collaborative conversations that outline the needs for specific types of professional development for staff and instructors in order to improve those strategic initiatives.
- Engage in collaborative conversations to identify what may be missing from the data gathered and whether that is acceptable given what we do and do not know about holistic learning and development.

In addition, we encourage instructors, staff, and administrators to do everything possible to ensure that the tests that may be selected by the accountability decision makers—whatever level on which they reside—are as good as they possibly can be. More important, community college educators need to discuss what the role of testing will be within comprehensive and holistic assessment efforts. Testing alone will not be sufficient to address the type of assessment efforts we have called for in this chapter because the postsecondary educational experience is much more than simple knowledge acquisition. Progressive community college leaders could begin to shape their future by calling for testing as a needed element of comprehensive assessment efforts, which include testing the cognitive and noncognitive preparedness levels of learners coming into community college by learning the goals of those students. Such a call may help to stay the efforts of those who would implement testing as the privileged, if not sole, means of assessing learning and holding community colleges accountable for student success. Further, by leading the response to the call for testing, progressive community college educators may be able to frame the content and design of tests. In light of our call for more holistic assessment, we would advocate the inclusion of elements such as Sedlacek's (1993) noncognitive variables; measures of student self-efficacy, attention, emotion, and cognitive regulation; the ability to self-refer; and questions regarding students' self-awareness of their strengths and limitations. Adding aspects such as these to measures of critical thinking or select sets of fundamental content would certainly make the future of testing much more palatable.

This approach to the future of testing is also consistent with the multiframe approach to leadership advocated by Bolman and Deal (2008) and utilized in this chapter. Testing itself is a scientific approach to the measurement of student learning—an approach consistent with the structural frame. Current debates regarding testing are more political because they reflect enduring differences, coalitions that include diverse stakeholders (including for-profit testing agencies), and negotiations related to the balance of funding and accountability. Absent are the human resources and symbolic frame perspectives. In terms of the former, calling for testing and participating in the design of tests could lead to instruments that are more culturally valid. This framework may place the tests in an appropriate context for educators and students, thus influencing fundamental motivations and relations between individuals and organizations. In terms of the symbolic frame, the participation of skeptical educators in the design of tests may influence perceptions and the meaning attributed to those tests. Rather than serving as hurdles or gatekeepers, tests could be framed as one form of data collection and used more as opportunities for students to learn about their strengths and growth areas. Thus, the inclusion of questions addressing learning preferences, self-awareness, and cultural strengths could help students to recognize that this is a different type of test. Better yet, if testing results are used to inform institutional assessment efforts rather than as prerequisites for a certificate or degree, students may approach the exams more expansively.

Our fundamental premise here is that the time may have passed for educators to proactively forgo the implementation of testing through the development of comprehensive assessment efforts, but there still is time for educators to influence the content, design, implementation, and use of tests within future holistic assessment efforts. That said, we feel that time is running out, and quickly. If community college educators continue to focus their time, energy, and efforts on resisting the inevitable future reality of testing, the window of opportunity to shape the future reality of testing may also pass. Once again, this is, at its core, a question of educational leadership more than it is a question of educational assessment.

Conclusion

We trust that you found plenty of ideas and strategies in the preceding chapters that will help you implement a sound outcomes-based assessment practice at your institution. We recognize that integrating your outcomes-based assessment processes into a holistic approach, as we recommend in this chapter, will mean making sure you have the practices in the preceding chapters implemented. And we recognize that it will also include a significant reallocation of time to collaborative conversations, planning, and prioritizing. We know that there is no such thing as "new time," and we recognize that many promotion, review, and tenure processes as well as collective bargaining agreements for instructors and staff do not include the time or even provide professional development for collaborating or learning new skills and knowledge to transform the design, delivery, and evaluation of postsecondary education. So, if you are looking for a place to begin beyond the implementation of the previous chapters' ideas, we recommend you review your hiring; collective bargaining; and promotion, review, and tenure processes to ensure that collaboration is a priority. Even if these processes are not revisited, no matter what, we recommend that you build in time to collaborate with all your constituents to learn how to collaborate and identify the times that collaboration will take place in everyone's workload. It is a simple and often overlooked concept of practice.

Next, we encourage you to move through the concepts presented in this chapter with diligence and care and urgency. We do not claim to have all the answers; however, what is clear: If we do not return to the holistic approach for student learning and development, we will segment the delivery and assessment of parcels of knowledge so much that the argument for modularized, nonfacilitated online learning (e.g., free online webinars, MOOCs) will look more and more affordable and more and more likely as the solution to reducing the cost of higher education. Would that be a bad idea? If the context for education within the community and two-year college is to educate the whole person, and to make education accessible to all while ensuring high-quality development of an adult learner who not only can stimulate the economy but do so in a manner that advances society and promotes global peace and well-being, then it seems to us a complete college experience is a wise choice for achieving this holistic approach. Research also tells us how this could become more likely true if we provide faculty and staff with the opportunity to design that type of environment. If you want to simply determine whether you graduated someone who has a set of knowledge acquisition at X-level, then the modularized, online system seems most affordable.

The urgency around the assessment and accountability conversation appears to present a fundamental challenge to institutional leadership. It appears that very few institutional leaders want to step forward with the evidence of what their students are learning and how they are developing. Why is that? Perhaps it is because their faculty cannot agree on what quality learning should look like and how it can be evaluated. Perhaps the answer is truly so complex it cannot be communicated in sound bites. Perhaps the American public and those holding institutional leadership accountable for such learning do not really want to know that when you do not invest in learning evidence of good learning declines. Perhaps no learning and development is occurring. Perhaps learning and development is occurring but the tools we are using to evaluate and report it are flawed.

It seems to us that the question is not, Where is the information about what students are learning and why can we not see it by state or by institutional type? The questions are, What does research tell us about how students learn and develop? And how well are we designing those opportunities for students to learn and develop within our organizations? What evidence do we have that we are implementing this research in educational systems? We can answer these questions. Research tells us that students learn and develop in ways that we do not currently fund. In other words, our financing of higher education does not match what we understand thus far from research with regard to how students learn and develop effectively. There is limited ability to design effective learning and development practices within institutions of higher education because there is limited investment in the designs of effective systems and processes. Why are we not investing in designing the most effective student learning and development opportunities for all students? Let us make sure the answer to *that* question has nothing to do with our lack of collecting the data to inform the conversation.

References

Alvarez, J. A., & Emory, E. (2006). Executive function and the frontal lobes: A meta-analytic review. *Neuropsychology Review, 16*(1), 17–42.

American College Personnel Association. (1994). *The student learning imperative: Implications for student affairs*. Washington, DC: Author.

Argyris, C., Putnam, R., & Smith, D. (1985). *Action science: Concepts, methods and skills for research and intervention.* San Francisco, CA: Jossey-Bass.

Barnard, C. I. (1938). *Functions of the executive.* Cambridge, MA: Harvard University Press.

Beer, M., Eisenstat, R., & Spector, B. (1990). Why change programs don't produce change. *Harvard Business Review, 68*(6), 158–166.

Bergquist, W. H., & Pawlak, K. (2008). *Engaging the six cultures of the academy.* San Francisco, CA: Jossey-Bass.

Bers, T. (2011). Program review and institutional effectiveness. *New Directions for Community Colleges, 153,* 63–73.

Bolman, L., & Deal, T. (1991). *Reframing organizations: Artistry, choice, and leadership.* San Francisco, CA: Jossey-Bass.

Bolman, L., & Deal, T. (1997). *Reframing organizations: Artistry, choice, and leadership* (2nd ed.). San Francisco, CA: Jossey-Bass.

Bolman, L., & Deal, T. (2003). *Reframing organizations: Artistry, choice, and leadership* (3rd ed.). San Francisco, CA: Jossey-Bass.

Bolman, L., & Deal, T. (2008). *Reframing organizations: Artistry, choice, and leadership* (4th ed.). San Francisco, CA: Jossey-Bass.

Bresciani, M. J. (2002). External partners in assessment of student development and learning. *New Directions for Student Services, 100,* 97–110.

Bresciani, M. J. (2006). *Outcomes-based academic and co-curricular program review.* Sterling, VA: Stylus.

Brock, T., Jenkins, D., Ellwein, T., Miller, J., Gooden, S., Martin, K, . . . Pih, M. (2007). *Building a culture of evidence for community college student success: Early progress in the Achieving the Dream Initiative.* New York, NY: MDRC. Retrieved November 18, 2007 from http://www.mdrc.org/publication/building-culture -evidence-community-college-student-success

Bush, G., Luu, P., & Posner, M. I. (2000). Cognitive and emotional influences in anterior cingulate cortex. *Trends in Cognitive Sciences, 4*(6), 215–223. task. *NeuroImage, 59,* 745–749.

Callahan, C. M. (2008, May 14). Assessment—our next call to action. *Net Results: Critical Issues for Student Affairs Practice.* Retrieved from: http://www.naspa.org

Carnevale, A. P., & Desrochers, D. M. (2004). Why learning? The value of higher education in society and the individual. In K. Boswell & C. D. Wilson (Eds.), *Keeping America's promise: A report on the future of the community college* (pp. 25–28). Denver, CO: Education Commission of the United States and League for Innovation. Retrieved July 8, 2008 from http://www.ecs.org/html/ Document.asp?chouseid=5309

Chan, R. C. K., Shum, D., Toulopoulou, T., & Chen, E. Y. H. (2008). Assessment of executive functions: Review of instruments and identification of critical issues. *Archives of Clinical Neuropsychology, 23*(2), 201–216.

Chiesa, A., Calati, R., & Serretti, A. (2011). Does mindfulness training improve cognitive abilities? A systematic review of neuropsychological findings. *Clinical Psychology Review, 31,* 449–464.

Clark, R. E., & Estes, F. (2002). *Turning research into results: A guide to selecting the right performance solutions.* Atlanta, GA: CEP Press.

Cyert, R. M., & March, J. G. (1959). A behavioral theory of organizational objectives. In M. Haire (Ed.), *Modern organization theory* (pp. 76–90). New York, NY: Wiley.

Dowd, A. C. (2005). *Data don't drive: Building a practitioner-driven culture of inquiry to assess community college performance.* Indianapolis, IN: Lumina Foundation for Education.

Fleming, J. (2002). Who will succeed in college? When the SAT predicts Black students' performance. *The Review of Higher Education, 25*(3), 281–296.

Fleming, J., & Garcia, N. (1998). Are standardized tests fair to African Americans? Predictive validity of the SAT in Black and White institutions. *The Journal of Higher Education, 69*(5), 471–495.

Galbraith, J. (2006). Matching strategy and structure. In J. V. Gallos (Ed.), *Organization development: A Jossey-Bass Reader* (pp. 565–582). San Francisco, CA: Jossey-Bass.

Goldin, C., & Katz, L. F. (2007). Long-run changes in the wage structure: Narrowing, widening, polarizing. *Brookings Papers on Economic Activity, 2*, 135–166.

Goldin, P. R., & Gross, J. J. (2010). Effects of mindfulness-based stress reduction (MBSR) on emotion regulation in social anxiety disorder. *Emotion, 10*(1), 83–91.

Hoffman, J. L. (2002). The impact of student cocurricular involvement on student success: Racial and religious differences. *Journal of College Student Development, 43*(5), 712–739.

Hoffman, J. L. (2010). An organization's search for meaning: A humanistic existential theory of organizational meaning and voice. *Journal of Psychological Issues in Organizational Culture, 1*(2), 40–63.

Hoffman, J. L., & Lowitzki, K. (2005). Predicting college success with high school grades and test scores: Limitations for minority students. *The Review of Higher Education, 28*(4), 455–474.

Hölzel, B. K., Carmody, J., Vangel, M., Congleton, C., Yerramsetti, S. M., Gard, T., & Lazar, S. W. (2011). Mindfulness practice leads to increases in regional brain gray matter density. *Psychiatry Research, 191*(1), 36–43.

Hölzel, B. K., Ott, U., Gard, T., Hempel, H., Weygandt, M., Morgen, K., & Vaitl, D. (2008). Investigation of mindfulness meditation practitioners with voxel-based morphometry. *Social Cognitive and Affective Neuroscience, 3*(1), 55–61.

Hölzel, B. K., Ott, U., Hempel, H., Hackl, A., Wolf, K., Stark, R., & Vaitl, D. (2007). Differential engagement of anterior cingulate and adjacent medial frontal cortex in adept meditators and non-meditators. *Neuroscience Letters, 421*(1), 16–21.

Hutcherson, C. A., Goldin, P. R., Ramel, W., McRae, K., & Gross, J. J. (2008). Attention and emotion influence the relationship between extraversion and neural response. *Social Cognitive and Affective Neuroscience, 3*(1), 71–79.

Jarvis, P. (1987). *Adult learning in the social context.* London, UK: Croom Helm.

Jencks, C., & Phillips, M. (1998). *The Black-White test score gap*. Washington, DC: Brookings Institution Press.

Kezar, A., & Eckel, P. D. (2002). The effect of institutional culture on change strategies in higher education. *The Journal of Higher Education, 73*(4), 435–460.

Kotter, J. P. (1995). Leading change: Why transformational efforts fail. *Harvard Business Review, 73*(2), 59–67.

Kozasa, E. H., et al. (2012). Meditation training increases brain efficiency in attention

Lazar, S. W., Kerr, C. E., Wasserman, R. H., Gray, J. R., Greve, D. N., Treadway, M. T., . . . Quinn, B. T. (2005). Meditation experience is associated with increased cortical thickness. *Neuroreport, 16*(17), 1893–1897.

Lutz, A., Slagter, H. A., Dunne, J. D., & Davidson, R. J. (2008). Attention regulation and monitoring in meditation. *Trends in Cognitive Sciences, 12*(4), 163–169.

Roueche, J. E., Johnson, L. F., & Roueche, S. D. (1997). *Embracing the tiger: The effectiveness debate and the community college*. Washington, DC: American Association of Community Colleges.

Schein, E. H. (2004). *Organizational culture and leadership* (3rd ed.). San Francisco, CA: Jossey-Bass.

Schein, E. H. (2006). So how can you assess your corporate culture? In J. V. Gallos (Ed.), *Organization development: A Jossey-Bass Reader* (pp. 614–633). San Francisco, CA: Jossey-Bass.

Scheurich, J. S., & Young, M. D. (1997). Coloring epistemologies: Are our research epistemologies racially biased? *Educational Researcher, 26*(4), 4–16.

Sedlacek, W. E. (1993). Employing noncognitive variables in admissions and retention in higher education. In L. Cortand (Ed.), *Achieving diversity: Issues in the recruitment and retention of underrepresented racial/ethnic students in higher education* (pp. 33–39). Alexandria, VA: National Association of College Admission Counselors.

Smart, J. C., Kuh, G. D., & Tierney, W. G. (1997). Roles of institutional cultures and decision approaches in promoting organizational effectiveness in two-year colleges. *The Journal of Higher Education, 68*, 256–281.

Todd, R. M., Cunningham, W. A., Anderson, A. K., & Thompson, E. (2012). Affect-biased attention as emotion regulation. *Trends in Sciences, 16*(7), 365–372.

Weinberg, S. (2012). *A designer universe?* Retrieved from http://www.physlink.com/education/essay_weinberg.cfm

Yosso, T. J. (2005). Whose culture has capital? A critical race theory discussion of community cultural wealth. *Race, Ethnicity, and Education, 8*(1), 69–91.

ABOUT THE CONTRIBUTORS

Jill Baker is dean of institutional effectiveness at San Diego Mesa College. She previously served as dean of the School of Business and Technology and as a member of the faculty. Prior leadership positions include faculty cochair and lead writer for accreditation, cochair of program review, internal consultant for strategic planning, and technology systems planning and administration. Jill has long been active in accreditation, including external evaluation team service. She currently teaches organization development as an adjunct professor for San Diego State University. Her research and professional interests include organizational culture and change, integrated planning, and building a culture of inquiry.

Julianna Barnes is vice president of student services at San Diego Mesa College. Previously she served as vice president of student services at Cuyamaca College, dean of student development and matriculation at San Diego City College, and dean of student affairs and matriculation at San Diego Miramar College. She formerly served as the acting executive director of Early Outreach and TRIO, TRIO Upward Bound director, outreach coordinator, and student affairs officer at University of California, San Diego. Julianna also serves as an affiliated member of the doctoral faculty at San Diego State University, and has served as an educational consultant to the Research and Planning Group (RP) as part of the Bridging Research Information and Cultures Initiative (BRIC), promoting cultures of inquiry in California community colleges.

Joy Battison has called Buffalo, New York, her home for the past eight years. She earned her master's degree in higher education and student affairs administration from Buffalo State College and plans to work with students who study abroad as well as with international students. Her goal is to help provide students with transformative learning experiences in order to create global citizens.

Marilee J. Bresciani is professor of postsecondary educational leadership at San Diego State University, where she teaches master's and doctoral students outcomes-based assessment and research methodology. She is also founder of the Rushing to Yoga Foundation, which seeks to increase understanding of integrative inquiry—the practice of exploring the unknown intuitive consciousness—and integrate it with evidence for processing within and outside of the postsecondary classroom.

Sandra Coyner is a professor of education in the Department of Educational Foundations and Leadership at The University of Akron. Sandra teaches courses in higher education in the areas of administration, curriculum, history, and organizational behavior. Her research and publication areas include assessment, college teaching and student learning, curriculum, and student populations including Saudi and Millennial students. Sandra's previous work experience includes serving as the director of assessment and accreditation for the College of Education and management positions in business and industry prior to joining the professoriate. Sandra currently serves as editor of *ATEA Journal*.

Paul A. Dale was appointed president of Paradise Valley Community College (PVCC) in Phoenix, Arizona, in March 2010. Previously he served two terms as interim president from 2008 to 2010 and during the 2003–4 academic year. He has also served PVCC as vice president of learning support services and dean of student services. In addition, Paul has served as an adjunct faculty member at Northern Arizona University and Arizona State University. He is especially interested in leadership development leading toward positive social change and has authored several book chapters on learning-centered college practices.

David P. Eppich has served as vice president for student services at San Juan College in Farmington, New Mexico, since July 2005. He came to San Juan College from Fort Lewis College in Durango, Colorado, where he most recently served as assistant to the president for external affairs. During his 25 years at Fort Lewis, David was director of developmental projects and special assistant to the president, director of the college union and student activities, and coach of the men's club soccer team. During his early career, he was manager of housing services and residence director at the University of New Mexico. David is active in economic development in the Four Corners, and formerly served as chair of the Colorado Region Nine Economic Development Board of Directors and chair of the board for the Colorado Association of Commerce and Industry. He has served the communities of Durango and Farmington in various capacities and been honored for his leadership by numerous organizations.

Sunday O. Faseyitan is currently dean of assessment projects at Butler County Community College, Butler, Pennsylvania. He leads the offices of Academic Assessment, Institutional Research, and Strategic Planning. In his role he designs assessment processes for institutional accountability and improvement and develops strategies to foster the cultivation of a culture of evidence among faculty and staff. Sunday is also a consultant evaluator to National Science Foundation grant recipients. Prior to his current position, Sunday taught engineering technology subjects at both two- and four-year colleges and has led engineering, science, and technology divisions as dean.

John Frederick is the director of learning outcomes assessment at Miami Dade College, Office of Institutional Effectiveness. He has a facilitative leadership role in working with various units of the college to plan, implement, and sustain their efforts in the assessment of student learning and continuous improvement.

John L. Hoffman is an associate professor of educational leadership at California State University, Fullerton, where he also serves as the director of the doctor of educational leadership program. Before transitioning to faculty, John spent 10 years working in administrative roles in academic and student affairs, 7 of which as a dean of students. He has experience in the development of theory-informed programs that enhance the success and retention of students of color, early interventions addressing student wellness and achievement, and the assessment of student learning in the cocurriculum. His research interests focus on assessment and accountability, professional competencies in student affairs and higher educational leadership, and professional development and mentoring.

Kimberly A. Kline is an associate professor of higher education administration at SUNY Buffalo State, where she currently teaches courses in assessment, tests and measurement, research methods in higher education, and moral reasoning in higher education. Her research and authored publications focus on professional development, issues of social justice/agency in higher education, and student learning outcomes assessment. Kim is interested in helping campuses develop grassroots efforts to promote student learning and development in higher education, and she has 20 years of experience in faculty and higher education/student affairs administration positions. Kim recently served as a Fulbright Scholar in Kyiv, Ukraine.

Megan Daane Lawrence has worked in higher education for 18 years, most recently as Heald College's senior director of institutional effectiveness, accreditation, and articulation at the San Francisco campus. Her primary responsibilities include working with administration, institutional research, student services, and faculty to facilitate the integration of program review, student learning outcome assessment, and strategic planning. She supports the college's regional accreditation through these efforts and has served as the college's accreditation liaison officer. She also facilitates transfer of Heald College course credit to local higher education institutions through articulation agreements. Prior to her current role, Megan managed Heald's career services, student services, and learning resource centers. She has also served as acting director of curriculum to facilitate faculty governance over Heald's academic programs and courses. Megan has more than five years' teaching experience at the college level both internationally and in the United States.

Victoria Livingston currently works as the assistant director of planning and assessment in the Division of Student Affairs & Enrollment Management at Northern Illinois University. She has served on the directorate board for the American College Personnel Association's Commission for Assessment & Evaluation since 2011. Her professional interests include assessment education and studying matters of inclusion and the intersection of identities.

Barbara Milliken began her career as an occupational therapist but transitioned to higher education in 1996. She is an associate professor who has taught in the occupational therapy assistant program at Stark State College, North Canton, Ohio, and now serves as department chair and program director. She has held administrative positions as an Ohio Skills Bank director and dean of corporate services and continuing education. Additionally, she serves as an institutional leader for faculty and staff professional development.

Megan Moore Gardner is an associate professor of higher education administration at the University of Akron. She currently teaches courses in assessment, higher education policy and accountability, organizational behavior, leadership in student affairs/services, and student development theory. Before transitioning to faculty, Megan spent a number of years working in administrative roles in student affairs. Her research focuses on a variety of topics including curricular and cocurricular assessment, professional development and accountability in higher education, Catholic higher education, and issues of social justice in higher education.

David Phillips is currently the academic testing coordinator at Borough of Manhattan Community College. His primary research interests include transnational higher education and its effect on access and foreign affairs.

Stacey N. Pierce is the current director of residential education at Hobart and William Smith Colleges in Geneva, New York. Her educational and career experiences have led her to institution types ranging from community college, public to private, small to large, and Division I colleges and universities. Stacey has worked in student affairs, specializing in residence life, student conduct, and student leadership for more than a decade. She strives to commit to assessment as an ongoing practice as opposed to a required event.

William E. Piland worked in the Fashion Merchandising Business before beginning a teaching career as a business teacher in community colleges. He held administrative positions as division director, dean of vocational education, and dean of instruction in Illinois community colleges. He was professor of education at Illinois State University for seven years. He taught postsecondary education leadership and workforce education courses at SDSU for 14 years.

Booker T. Piper, Jr. earned his master's degree in higher education administration at SUNY Buffalo State. Prior to completing his graduate work, Booker served two years in the Army National Guard as a combat engineer. He also taught high school Earth science for four years in the Buffalo public school system. Booker's research focuses on minority male and nontraditional student learning, development, and retention practices.

Thomas C. Priester serves as the instructor of transitional studies at Genesee Community College, Batavia, New York. He previously worked in the areas of academic success, student life, student leadership development, orientation, academic advising, and residence life. In his current position, Tom is also an adviser to Phi Theta Kappa, the chairperson of the Transitional Studies committee, and he sits on the campuswide Academic Assessment committee. Tom also teaches for the Higher Education Student Affairs Administration graduate program at SUNY Buffalo State College in Buffalo, New York, and taught at the Attica Correctional Facility in Attica, New York, as well as at Fatec Americana in Brazil. His research interests include the study of developmental education at the community college and the study of hope in community college students.

Barbara June Rodriguez has more than 15 years of experience in higher education at community colleges in North Carolina and Florida. She started her career as a community college English instructor and has served in administrative positions within academic affairs and student services. Barbara remains engaged in teaching and learning as an adjunct English professor. Her research and professional interests are outcomes-based assessment and accreditation. She currently serves as the director of the Quality Enhancement Plan at Broward College in Florida.

Stephanie Romano has nearly 25 years of experience in training and education. She started her career as an instructor, a curriculum developer, and a manager in corporate training settings. Stephanie moved into career-focused higher education in 2003 and joined Alta Colleges, where she was ultimately responsible for the design, development, and management of more than 30 accredited residential and online degree programs. She then joined Heald College in 2007. There, as director of curriculum and later as vice president of curriculum and instruction, she was responsible for managing academic programs, curriculum development, faculty development, and learning resource centers throughout the 12-campus, regionally accredited college. In that capacity, Stephanie, in partnership with the director of institutional effectiveness, played an integral role in the development of the institution's program review and student learning outcomes assessment model. Stephanie is currently the director of Hybrid and Blended Learning for Education Affiliates.

Virginia (Ginny) Taylor is currently serving as vice president for student and enrollment services at Genesee Community College (GCC) in Batavia, New York. This appointment followed a seven-year stretch at GCC as dean of enrollment management. Previous to these appointments, Ginny spent almost 15 years at Niagara County Community College, where she worked as an admissions recruiter, an orientation leader, an academic adviser, a nontraditional program(s) coordinator, and a college success and career planning instructor. In addition, she held directorships in cooperative education, tech-prep/school-to-work, financial aid, and enrollment services. She is also currently serving as an adjunct professor at the State University of New York at Buffalo and Niagara University.